Key Figures in Counselling and Psychotherapy

Series editor: Windy Dryden

The *Key Figures in Counselling and Psychotherapy* series of books provides a concise, accessible introduction to the lives, contributions and influence of the leading innovators whose theoretical and practical work has had a profound impact on counselling and psychotherapy. The series includes comprehensive overviews of:

Sigmund Freud
by Michael Jacobs

Eric Berne
by Ian Stewart

Carl Rogers
by Brian Thorne

C A R L

Rogers

BRIAN THORNE

SAGE Publications
London • Newbury Park • New Delhi

First published 1992. Reprinted 1992

SAGE Publications Ltd
6 Bonhill Street
London EC2A 4PU

SAGE Publications Inc
2455 Teller Road
Newbury Park, California 91320

SAGE Publications India Pvt Ltd
32, M-Block Market
Greater Kailash – I
New Delhi 110 048

British Library Cataloguing in Publication Data
Thorne, Brian
    Carl Rogers. (Key Figures in
    Counselling & Psychotherapy Series)
    I. Title   II. Series
    150.92

    ISBN 0–8039–8462–6
    ISBN 0–8039–8463–4 (pbk)

Library of Congress catalog card number 91-051203

Typeset by Mayhew Typesetting, Rhayader, Powys
Printed in Great Britain by J. W. Arrowsmith Ltd, Bristol

Contents

'I can trust my experience'
Carl Rogers

For Christine, Julian, Mary and Clare
for tolerating my absences

For Christine and Rosalind
for tolerating my handwriting

Preface

Carl Rogers enabled countless people throughout the world to be themselves with confidence. His impact has been enormous through his voluminous writings, through the school of counselling and psychotherapy which he founded and through the indirect influence of his work on many areas of professional activity where the quality of human relationships is central. And yet he was always suspicious of those who sought power and he eschewed every attempt to make him into a guru figure. He believed deeply in the capacity of every individual to find his or her own way forward and, as a result, he not infrequently adopted a self-effacing attitude which for the less discerning concealed his greatness. The best facilitator, he maintained, was the one who enabled others to feel that they had done it themselves, whatever 'it' might be.

This small book attempts to convey the essence of Rogers' theoretical ideas about the nature of human beings and about what happens in effective therapeutic relationships. It also gives an insight into Rogers' actual way of working with people in therapy and draws out the practical implications of what is, in effect, a functional philosophy of human growth and relationships. Rogers, gentle and courteous as he usually was, made enemies because his ideas and way of being tend to threaten those whose self-esteem is dependent on their professional expertise or their capacity to impose a particular perception of reality on others. Both among fellow psychologists and those from other disciplines he was sometimes seen as naive, utopian and perversely misguided in his optimistic view of human potential. Some of his critics undoubtedly raise serious questions about the validity of his approach and in Chapter 4 I attempt to explore the more telling of these objections and to refute them where possible. Rogers himself, however, never claimed that he had established the absolute truth about anything; indeed he was committed to a ceaseless process of learning and held to the temporariness of all knowledge. For him the mark of the mature person was a fearless openness to both inner and outer experience, however disturbing this might prove to previously held convictions.

I was privileged to know Rogers during the last ten years of his life and to work with him on a number of occasions in different parts of the world. The biographical chapter with which the book opens owes little, however, to my direct involvement with him. Most of the content is distilled from Rogers' own writings, from Howard Kirschenbaum's outstanding biography, *On Becoming Carl Rogers* (1979) and from the summary of Rogers' life provided by David Cain, editor of the *Person-Centered Review*, in Vol. 2 No.4 (1987) of the journal which served the person-centred community well in the immediate years after Rogers' death in February 1987. I trust these two men will forgive my plundering of their dedicated research into Rogers' life and work.

In one respect this book may perhaps claim some originality. Unlike many of my colleagues in the field of person-centred or client-centred therapy, I see in Rogers and his work the re-emergence of a spiritual tradition which has its origins in the early writers of the Old Testament and continues through Jesus, the earliest Christian theologians and many of the great medieval writers, not least Dame Julian of Norwich, much loved and honoured in the city where I live and work. This tradition is acutely conscious of the divine indwelling within the created universe and in each human being. It bears witness to the uncondi-tionality of the love which is poured out by God on his creation and to the capacity of human beings to internalize that love and then to give it expression in their relating. Rogers died an agnostic but in his later years his openness to experience compelled him to acknowledge the existence of a dimension to which he attached such adjectives as mystical, spiritual and transcendental. In many ways he often provides the channel into spiritual experience for secular men and women who have long since rejected the idea of God and the trappings of institutional religion and he does so by enabling them to discover the infinite worth and uniqueness of their own being. Yet with this recognition of personal value there comes an accompanying sense of interconnectedness with other human beings and with the whole of the created order. In short, Rogers does not provide, as some have suggested, the mirror for Narcissus but the assurance and acceptance of individual uniqueness and the invitation to communion. Given a different theology in his childhood and adolescence, it is not over-fanciful to suppose that Rogers might himself have become a much-loved pastor and theologian whose life could have transformed the face of the Church. An underlying theme in this book, however, is that God moves in a mysterious way and that client-centred therapy and the person-centred approach will continue to contribute to the psychological and spiritual well-being of humanity to a degree which would have been impossible if Rogers had not turned his back on Christianity and the Church in order to find a greater freedom.

Many people have encouraged me in the writing of the book but I am particularly indebted to my colleagues in the University of East Anglia, the Norwich Centre and Person-centred Therapy (Britain) for their support and the stimulation they have offered, often in the midst of frenetic lives characterized by an ever-escalating clientele. I am grateful to the University for granting me a brief period of study leave in the summer of 1991 and to my Norwich Centre partners for convincing me that I should not feel guilty about writing books instead of seeing yet more clients in order to ensure the Centre's financial security. To Maria Bowen, Rogers' close friend and colleague at the Center for Studies of the Person in La Jolla, my debt is inestimable for she not only encouraged me in the project but also provided me with invaluable material from her own long experience of sharing in Rogers' work and aspirations. I only hope the result will serve to make Rogers' immense contribution more accessible to those to whom he is little more than a name in psychology textbooks. I hope, too, that in a small way it will help to ensure the continuing health and development of person-centred therapy in a world which all too often seems to sacrifice persons on the altars of efficiency, expediency or the latest version of the market economy.

Brian Thorne
Norwich 1991

Acknowledgements

The author and publishers would like to thank the following for permission to reproduce copyright extracts from the sources shown:

1 American Psychological Association: 'A Note on the Nature of Man', C.R. Rogers, *Journal of Counseling Psychology*, 4(3), 1957 and 'In Retrospect: Forty-Six Years', C.R. Rogers, *American Psychologist*, 29(2), 1974;

2 Houghton Mifflin Company: *Counseling and Psychotherapy*, C.R. Rogers (1942); *On Becoming a Person*, C.R. Rogers (1961) and *A Way of Being*, C.R. Rogers (1980);

3 Jossey-Bass Inc.: *Psychotherapist's Casebook*, eds I.L. Kutash and A. Wolf (1986);

4 Howard Kirschenbaum: *On Becoming Carl Rogers* (1979). New York: Delacorte Press;

5 Leuven University Press: *Client-Centered and Experiential Psychotherapy in the Nineties*, eds G. Lietaer, J. Rombauts and R. Van Balen (1990);

6 McGraw-Hill Inc.: *Psychology: A Study of Science, Vol III*, ed. S. Koch (1959);

7 Bernie Neville: Unpublished manuscript, 'Rogers, Jung and the Post-modern Condition', 1991;

8 Sage Publications Inc. for extracts from the *Person-centered Review*.

9 Constable & Co., Ltd for extracts from *The Carl Rogers Reader*, eds H. Kirschenbaum and V.L. Henderson (1990) and *Carl Rogers: Dialogues*, eds H. Kirschenbaum and V.L. Henderson (1990).

Every effort has been made to obtain permission to reproduce copyright material throughout this book. If any proper acknowledgement has not been made, or permission not received, we would invite any copyright holder to inform us of this oversight and the necessary arrangements will be made at the first opportunity.

1

The Life of Carl Rogers

Childhood and Adolescence

Carl Ransom Rogers was born on 8 January 1902 in a suburb of Chicago called Oak Park. He was the fourth of six children, five of whom were boys, and the family could trace its roots far back into United States history. Rogers' father, Walter, was a graduate of the University of Wisconsin at a time when college education was not widespread, and when Carl was born he had already established himself as an up and coming businessman in the engineering field. Carl's mother, Julia, had also attended college for two years and, like her husband, she came from a family which had first crossed the Atlantic in the seventeenth century and had made notable contributions to the community and to the development of the new country over more than 300 years. Carl Rogers was not, then, a European emigrant like so many of his well-known contemporaries in the world of American psychology but a genuine product of Midwestern America. The pioneering and pragmatic spirit of his ancestors was a significant part of his inheritance.

Rogers was later to describe his home as a place marked by close family ties and permeated by a religious and ethical atmosphere which was strict and brooked no compromise (Rogers, 1961: 6). Undoubtedly he was loved but the almost excessive attention to the children's welfare exhibited by Walter and Julia Rogers was accompanied by a subtle and affectionate control which was based on an almost fundamentalist approach to Christianity and on the worship of the virtue of hard work. It was a basic assumption in the Rogers household that the family was different from other people and consequently they observed standards of behaviour appropriate to those who were of the 'elect' of God. No drinking of alcohol was permitted, no dancing or theatre visits, no card games and, indeed, little social life of any kind. Instead there was an emphasis on a close-knit family life and on the necessity of much work at all times.

Carl's health as a boy was not good and he was perceived by the rest of the family as a somewhat sickly child who was prone to be over-sensitive. This sometimes led to teasing banter which could verge on cruelty and exacerbated a tendency on Carl's part to retreat into himself and into his own fantasy world. He often spoke of himself as a lonely child who was permitted few opportunities to make friends outside the family and who was driven more and more to seek consolation in books, which he read incessantly. When he began formal schooling he was already reading at a standard several years in advance of his age and this ability further distanced him from his contemporaries. Even at this early stage of his life it is possible to see the beginnings of the disciplined and conscientious scholar who nonetheless yearned for an intimacy of which the family culture deprived him.

In 1914 the family moved to a large farm thirty miles to the west of Chicago. Reflecting on the move later, Rogers saw it as motivated by two different factors. In the first place, his father, now a successful and prosperous businessman, wanted a farm for a hobby but Carl came to believe that the second and more important reason was a desire on the part of his parents to protect their growing adolescent children from the 'temptations' of suburban city life (Rogers, 1961: 6). The social isolation thus continued for Carl throughout his secondary schooling and he ruefully admits that he went through high school with only two dates to his credit. Life on the farm, however, enabled him to develop interests which were to have significance in his later professional life. The lonely, somewhat introverted adolescent became totally fascinated by the great night-flying moths which inhabited the woods around the farm. Gradually he became an authority on these exotic creatures, read about them extensively and, most significantly, began himself to breed the moths in captivity, reared the caterpillars and watched over the cocoons during the long winter months. In this adolescent enthusiasm it is not difficult to see the emerging scientist who was learning what it means to wait patiently for nature to reveal her secrets. The scientific bent was further encouraged by Walter Rogers' determination to operate his new farm on as scientific a basis as possible. He challenged his sons to set up small independent ventures of their own and, as a result, they learned to manage flocks of chickens and to rear many varieties of farm livestock from infancy. Carl through this activity became an assiduous student of scientific agriculture and learned through his reading of a voluminous tome called *Feeds and Feeding* by Morison what was entailed in setting up valid experiments. It was here that he first understood what was meant by experimental and control groups and became familiar with randomizing procedures. In short, he acquired a knowledge of and a great respect for scientific methodology and realized from first-hand experience how difficult it is to test a hypothesis. He also discovered that with his moths and agricultural experiments he could experience intense pleasure and satisfaction and could, to some extent at least, forget the deeper yearning for human intimacy.

Student Days

New Freedom

With such a background it is scarcely surprising that when, following the family tradition, Rogers became a student at the University of Wisconsin, he should enrol in the field of scientific agriculture. His ambition at this stage was to manage a farm in the most modern and scientific fashion possible. In fact he was embarking upon a period of profound personal change and development. He shared a room with his brother, Ross, at the YMCA dormitory and in his first year he became a member of a Sunday morning group of agricultural students led by Professor George Humphrey. The impact of this group was enormous for a number of reasons. It is evident that Humphrey was unusual in so far as he encouraged the group to make its own decisions and refused to adopt a conventional leadership role. Rogers himself was later to describe the experience in glowing terms and referred to Humphrey's behaviour as 'an excellent example of facilitative leadership' (in Burton, 1972: 36). The difference in style and intention from the benign but controlling influence of Rogers' parents could scarcely have been greater and he was deeply affected by the liberation of thought and feeling that followed. What is more, he was enabled for the first time to develop close and intimate relationships with young people from outside the immediate family circle and this, too, opened up for him a whole new world of exciting possibilities. The upsurge of intellectual and emotional energy needed a new channel and Rogers' emerging idealism soon led him to focus on his Christian commitment. Before the end of his sophomore year he felt firmly convinced that he was called to be a Christian minister and he accordingly changed his major from agriculture to history in the belief that the latter would provide him with a more appropriate background for religious work. For a young man whose best subjects at school had been science and English and who received straight A grades in almost all his courses, the transition presented no intellectual difficulties. More significant was the nature of the religious transformation which was taking place. The dogmatic and moralistic Christianity of Rogers' home environment was giving way to an altogether more passionate and personal involvement based on a changing perception of the nature of Christ. It is scarcely an exaggeration to deduce from a reading of Rogers' diaries and letters of this time that the judgemental and awesome God of the Old Testament was gradually being replaced in Rogers' experience by a vibrantly human Jesus who offered a new intimacy and extended the possibility of a personal freedom which would have been inconceivable in the context of the evangelical fundamentalism with which Rogers had grown up.

Journey to China

In the midst of this sea-change of religious perception Rogers was chosen as one of only a dozen students from the United States to attend a World Student Christian Federation conference in Peking, China. This tour was to last more than six months and was a watershed in Rogers' spiritual and intellectual development. We have a detailed record of his experience for he assiduously maintained a 'China diary' and wrote lengthy letters throughout the trip both to his family and to Helen Elliot, a girl he had known since childhood and whom he now regarded as his 'sweetheart'. The situation could hardly have been more conducive to the development of a young man's personal autonomy for there was not only the stimulus of foreign travel and the experience of a totally different culture but also the constant company of an international group of highly intelligent and creative young people. Rogers was forced to stretch his thinking in almost all directions and was also brought poignantly to face the power of national feelings and bitterness in a period only a few years after the end of World War I. Most significantly he came to recognize that it was possible for sincere and honest people to hold very different religious beliefs and perceptions.

Looking back on the whole experience Rogers realized that it was for him the perfect context in which to break free of the religious thinking of his parents and to achieve spiritual, intellectual and emotional independence. Throughout he was sustained by his new and deeply personal relationship with Christ and by the fact that he was, through letters, becoming increasingly intimate with Helen. Not the least astonishing aspect of this period was Rogers' faithful recording of his new feelings and ideas in immensely detailed letters to his family. It would seem that he was compelled to be honest and that this compulsion blinded him temporarily to the effect that such letters would inevitably have on his parents, who were deeply distressed and even scandalized by their son's embracing of what they must have considered a dangerous and perverse theology. To add to this, they could make no immediate reply, and by the time their negative reactions caught up with him Rogers was fully established in his new outlook. As he later admitted, it was through this process that, with the minimum of pain to himself, he broke with intellectual and religious ties which could have proved formidably strong. It is possible to see in this fascinating journey to the East the early indicators of much that was to characterize Rogers' later life and work. As he experienced the depth of group life so it became possible for him to understand and to value individual differences. What is more the acceptance he found in the group, the increasing security of the relationship with Helen and his changing perception of the nature of God enabled him to maintain an authenticity which was crucial to his escape from the shackles of the narrow parental view of reality. The interweaving of the later core conditions of empathy, acceptance and genuineness is not difficult to trace.

Marriage
The China tour took its toll on Rogers' physical health and something of the stress it engendered is revealed by the fact that shortly after his return he was diagnosed as having a duodenal ulcer. He was hospitalized for a few weeks and then returned home for further treatment and a period of convalescence. If the changes that had taken place had not been radical it is easy to imagine that this period of vulnerability could have posed a real threat to Rogers' newly won autonomy. It is a mark of his determination that this should not happen that, as soon as he was fit enough, he took a job at a lumberyard and registered for a correspondence course in introductory psychology where the principal text was by William James. The time of his recuperation also provided an admirable opportunity for deepening his relationship with Helen, who was an art student at the University of Wisconsin. He bought his first car (a used Model T Ford) and frequently drove twenty-five miles over rough roads in order to be with the girl whom he described in words which leave little doubt that he was falling ever more deeply in love. In time, his feelings were reciprocated and the day arrived when, in his own words, 'the most wonderful miracle in the world took place' and Helen told him that she loved him. They were engaged on 9 October 1922; Rogers considered the event to be one of the peak experiences of his life and described himself as 'ecstatically happy'. They were married in August 1924 only two months after Rogers graduated in history from the

University of Wisconsin. The marriage took place despite the urgings from the parents of both families to postpone the event until they were more firmly established in their respective careers. Rogers had been accepted by Union Theological Seminary in New York, the most liberal in the country at that time, and soon after their marriage the young couple piled the totality of their worldly possessions into a second-hand Model T coupé that Rogers had bought for 450 dollars and set out for New York.

From Theology to Psychology
When Rogers began his studies at Union he was still intent on becoming a Christian minister and during the summer of his first year, as part of his seminary training, he acted as the pastor of a small church in Vermont. His offerings were apparently scholarly enough but he found it quite beyond him to preach for longer than twenty minutes – this in the days when sermons of forty minutes or an hour were not uncommon. The reluctance to impose his view on others and his distaste for telling others what they should do or believe is already evident in this somewhat amusing shortcoming of the fledgling seminarian.

Rogers never regretted the two years he spent at Union. He met some exceptional teachers and participated fully in the life of an institution which was remarkably progressive in its attitudes to learning and to student demands and aspirations. Despite this, Rogers and some of his fellow students grew restless at what they considered to be the imparting of ideas *ex cathedra* and made the remarkable request of the administration that they should be permitted to set up a seminar, for credit, with no instructors, where the agenda should be composed entirely of their own questions. Even more remarkably their request was granted, although the Seminary administration did insist that a young instructor should sit in on their meetings even if he took no active part in the proceedings. For Rogers, as for the others involved, this 'leaderless' seminar proved to be deeply clarifying and broke much new ground. So disturbing was the outcome that most of the participants, in facing honestly the questions which they raised, thought themselves right out of religious work. Once again Rogers was thrown into creative confusion. He later wrote that increasingly he came to realize that, deeply as he was committed to the constructive improvement of life for society and for individuals, he could not stay in a field where he would be *required* to believe in a specific religious doctrine. The thought of *having* to profess a set of beliefs in order to remain in one's profession struck Rogers as something to which he applied an adjective of great emotional force. Such a prospect, he said, was 'horrible' (Rogers, 1961: 8).

Rogers' restlessness with his religious studies was already evident during his second year at Union and he found an outlet by taking several courses at the neighbouring Teachers' College of Columbia University. By simply walking across the road he found himself following a course in clinical psychology under the guidance of Leta Hollingworth, of whom he significantly remarked that she combined the qualities of a warm human being with those of a competent research worker. It was thanks to Hollingworth that he had his first experience of working with disturbed children. Equally important was his contact with William Heard Kilpatrick who was a former student of John Dewey and expounded Dewey's views on progressive education with great power and persuasiveness. When, therefore, thanks to the processes of the leaderless seminar, Rogers came finally to acknowledge that he could no longer remain in a religious milieu it was not difficult to decide where to go. Instead of making frequent visits to Teachers' College, he once more crossed the road and asked for permanent residence. The graduate who had set out to become a Christian minister now embarked on the career of psychologist and it says much for the health and flexibility of the American higher education system of that time that the transition was accomplished with the minimum of bureaucratic difficulty.

In the same year that Rogers began to study for his degree in clinical and educational psychology at Teachers' College, he became a father for the first time. David Rogers was born on 17 March 1926 and it is amusing to record that Carl and Helen initially set out to raise their first-born son according to the book of Watsonian behaviourism. Rogers was later to write that it was fortunate for them all that Helen had enough common sense to make a good mother in the face of all the seemingly erudite but essentially damaging psychological knowledge (in Burton, 1972: 44). At Teachers' College Rogers found that the predominating point of view was characterized by a rigorous scientific approach allied to a coldly objective statistical methodology. This appealed at some level to the scientific part of his personality and his own doctoral work consisted of developing a test for measuring the personality adjustment of 9–13-year-old children (a test which proved immensely popular and was still selling well in the 1970s). The interest in working with children led Rogers to apply successfully for a Fellowship at the Institute of Child Guidance and for the academic year 1927–8 he had the opportunity to experience an entirely different milieu from that of Teachers' College. The Institute was largely committed to psychoanalytic theory and

methods and Rogers found himself surrounded by clinical practitioners whose orientation was radically different to that of most of
his tutors at Teachers'. It would seem that Rogers drew
considerable benefit from this contrast of approaches for, in the
event, he felt comfortable with neither but was able to draw from
both. Fascinatingly, the personality test that emerged from his
doctoral studies satisfied the scientific objectivity of his examiners
at Teachers' College and was also deemed useful as a clinical
instrument at the Institute. Already we see in this test his concern
to tap into the subjective experiencing of his client, for the children
taking the test were enabled to explore their attitudes to
themselves, their contemporaries and their families and to do this
through the context of their daydreams and fantasy life.

The Rochester Years

Rogers' inability or unwillingness to throw in his lot with any of
the prevailing psychological 'orthodoxies' of the time is an indication of the independence of spirit which also characterized the
choice of his first professional post as a psychologist. In the spring
of 1928 he accepted a position with the Child Study Department
of the Rochester Society for the Prevention of Cruelty to Children.
It was poorly paid and seemed to have little in the way of career
prospects. Indeed, it would cut him off from the intellectual
stimulus of university life and commit him to an unfashionable area
of work. Yet for Rogers the choice seems to have been largely
intuitive and spontaneous. The post offered the prospect of work
which he enjoyed and for which his training equipped him. For
him this was enough and, characteristically, he followed his
instinct and trusted his own inner sense of conviction about the
rightness of the move. This mode of operating is not without
significance for someone who was later to place such emphasis on
the person's trust in his or her own internal 'locus of evaluation'
when making decisions or evaluating situations of emotional
complexity.

Rogers later described the next twelve years in Rochester as
exceedingly valuable ones. He was totally immersed in his work
and dedicated himself unstintingly to the welfare of the maladjusted and often highly deprived children who were referred to
him for diagnosis and assistance. The fact that many of the
children were badly damaged and had often been through the
rigours of the courts and social work agencies meant that there was
little time for testing out elaborate theories and hypotheses. Instead
what was required was a method of responding to the children and

their parents which actually worked and proved effective in meeting their needs. In such a pressurized situation Rogers soon discovered that even some of the most elegant theories he had previously embraced failed to stand up to the test of reality. More and more he began to realize that he could regard himself as a pioneer in his own right and that he could take the risk of formulating his own ideas based on the day-to-day experience of the encounters he was having with those seeking his help.

This essentially practical and pragmatic approach was reinforced by the enthusiasm and energy of some of the social workers working in Rogers' department. Notable among them was Elizabeth Davis who was a student of the Freudian heretic, Otto Rank, and had been trained at the University of Pennsylvania School of Social Work. Rogers was also much affected by the work of Rank's student, Jessie Taft. She and her colleague, Frederick Allen, became a major influence in Rogers' professional life and it was their version of Rank's ideas and practice which gradually permeated Rogers' own thinking and clinical behaviour. It was only many years later that Rogers openly acknowledged his indebtedness to Jessie Taft and spoke of being at this time 'infected with Rankian ideas'. His biographer, Howard Kirschenbaum, records how in an interview Rogers stated that it was at this time that he began 'to realize the possibilities of the individual being self directing'. Rogers went on to link the influence of Rank with his previous exposure to the ideas of Kilpatrick and John Dewey (Kirschenbaum, 1979: 95). It was probably at Rochester that Rogers came to believe in the individual's capacity to find his or her own way forward and this belief, it seems, was primarily founded on his clinical experience but buttressed by his understanding of Rank's work as it was transmitted to him by the words and example of Jessie Taft and her colleagues. It was also in the later years at Rochester that he finally accepted the comparative ineffectiveness therapeutically of interpreting a client's behaviour. It was at this time that the now famous incident occurred when Rogers finally gave up on a delinquent youngster's mother who had constantly refused to accept his gentle interpretations of her behaviour towards her son only to be asked a moment or two later by the same woman if he actually took on adults for counselling. When he said he did she then began her story all over again in her own way and talked about her despair and her marital relationship, which was in serious trouble. For Rogers this proved conclusively that it is the client who knows how to proceed and not the therapist and that the therapist's task is to rely upon the client for the direction of therapeutic movement.

While he was still at Rochester Rogers wrote his first major book, *The Clinical Treatment of the Problem Child*, which was published in 1939. The book attempted to give something of an overview of the field of child guidance during that period but its interest now lies more in the insight it provides into Rogers' own personal and professional growth. As Kirschenbaum points out, the book contained the seeds of much of what was to follow in the years ahead and he draws attention particularly to the sections that consider the role of the therapist and the place of scientific research (Kirschenbaum, 1979: 96).

Having considered the different types of therapy with which he had worked at Rochester, Rogers concluded that to some extent they converged in the attitude of the therapist. He went on to identify four basic attributes of all therapists and listed these as:

1 *objectivity*, in which he included a 'capacity for sympathy which will not be overdone, a genuinely receptive and interested attitude, a deep understanding which will find it impossible to pass moral judgements or be shocked and horrified'.
2 *a respect for the individual*: 'the aim is to leave the major responsibilities in the hands of the child as an individual going towards independence'.
3 *understanding of the self*, to which he allied the therapist's ability to be self-accepting as well as self-aware.
4 *psychological knowledge*, by which he meant 'a thorough basis of knowledge of human behaviour and of its physical, social and psychological determinants'. (Rogers, 1939)

It is significant that for Rogers at this time the first three of these attributes far outweighed the fourth in importance. Knowledge allied to a brilliant intellect was no guarantee of therapeutic effectiveness and he is clear that it is in the realm of 'attitudes, emotions and insights' that the therapist's essential capacity is determined. Once again we can see the roots of empathy, unconditional positive regard and congruence, the three concepts which were to become Rogers' most important and radical contribution to the understanding of helping relationships (Rogers, 1939: 279–84).

Rogers' concern with the importance of scientific research was by no means a commonly held point of view at this time. Kirschenbaum suggests that for many practitioners the time was not yet ripe for research because therapy was still in its infancy. Others, again, including the persuasive Jessie Taft, were doubtful that science could usefully be applied to therapy at all. Rogers strongly disagreed with these views although he confessed that for him it was a 'horrible thought' that the day might come when therapeutic processes could actually be measured. Nonetheless he insisted that it was the psychologist's duty to prevent therapy from taking off into a kind of mystical stratosphere and that it should be firmly anchored in the domain of scientific enquiry and thus be brought down to earth (Kirschenbaum, 1979: 98). The use of the adjective 'horrible' reminds us of Rogers' previous revulsion at the thought of being trapped in a profession (the Christian ministry) because he had to give allegiance to a certain belief structure. It would seem that, committed scientist that he was, Rogers still feared another kind of trap; the possibility that everything might one day be explicable in scientific terms. It was as if he believed that the psychologist should certainly attempt to bring this about but that it would be a tragic day if he actually succeeded. This commitment to scientific enquiry allied to a basic ambivalence about its ultimate efficacy constitutes a somewhat uneasy tension which persisted at some level throughout Rogers' life and continues to be observable among person-centred therapists since his death.

Rogers was sure that he owed his next post solely to the publication of *Clinical Treatment of the Problem Child*. Without his ability to write quickly and persuasively in the occasional intervals in his frenetic clinical life, he might have continued for many years in Rochester, where he was eventually appointed director of the Guidance Center. As it was, he was startled and delighted to be offered a full professorship at Ohio State University and in December 1939 he and his young family set out in a blizzard for their new home.

The Ohio State Professor

Rogers later commented that he heartily recommended starting in the academic world at the professorial level (Rogers, 1961: 13). For those less fortunate who had to work their way up through the ranks of university faculty there was always the need to keep in favour in order to ensure promotion. Rogers was not constrained in this way and from the outset of his time at Ohio State he was able to be exceptionally active and innovative. He lectured frequently, published numerous articles within his first year, served on countless committees and established a practicum in counselling and psychotherapy which meant that supervised therapy was carried out on a university campus for the first time. Within this stimulating context and with the encouragement of his many and enthusiastic students it was not long before Rogers came to realize that his already extensive experience had brought him to the point where he was rapidly developing a distinctive viewpoint of his own which was demanding more extensive articulation. On 11

December 1940, before an invited audience at the University of Minnesota, he delivered a lecture entitled 'Newer concepts in psychotherapy' and he subsequently came to consider the date of this event as the birthday of client-centred therapy. Kirschenbaum in his biography of Rogers draws attention both to the content of this lecture and to the context in which it was delivered (Kirschenbaum, 1979: 112–13). The relevance of the latter lies in the light that it throws upon the personality of Rogers, although I am not sure that I concur with Kirschenbaum's assessment of the event.

The well-known counselling programme for student personnel workers at Minnesota had been developed under the leadership of Dean E. G. Williamson, who believed in a distinctly directive approach which included the use of psychological tests and focused advice-giving. It was to Williamson's students and associates that Rogers gave his lecture. Much of the paper was devoted to a detailed critique of the more traditional approaches to therapy and he was particularly harsh on the practice of advice-giving. To illustrate his thesis Rogers at one point quoted from the record of an interview conducted by an advice-giving counsellor, but neglected to tell his audience that the counsellor in question was none other than the chairman of the very meeting at which he was speaking. In short, Rogers had gone to the foremost citadel of directive therapy and there delivered a powerful attack on the 'home team's' theories and practice using the chairman's own performance as a principal target for his assault. Kirschenbaum describes this astonishing demonstration of personal and professional courage as Rogers 'naively' going to present his paper. Perhaps he is right, for it seems that Rogers was unprepared for the furore which his paper aroused but I find it difficult to believe that Rogers did not realize at some level that he was carrying out a revolutionary act. His later development shows him to have been a skilled political animal with a sure nose for the effective strategy, and although he preferred to be seen as a 'quiet revolutionary' I have little doubt that he went to Minnesota in December 1940 knowing that he had something of a time bomb in his briefcase.

Having launched his critique of the older methods of therapy, Rogers goes on in the paper to describe the 'newer practices'. He gives due credit to the influence of Rank, Jessie Taft and Frederick Allen and alludes, too, to the work of Karen Horney and to the emerging fields of play therapy and group therapy. He then stresses that the new approach is not interested in solving problems but rather in helping individuals to grow and develop so that they can have a more integrated response to life in general. Further key issues he explores include the emphasis on feelings and emotions rather than on cognitive aspects of a situation, the focus on the present rather than the past and the crucial experience of the therapeutic relationship itself as a major element in the growth of the client.

The reception of the paper, which varied from enthusiastic approval to somewhat aggressive criticism, convinced Rogers that he was saying something new and not simply summarizing or synthesizing the work of others. He embarked on a second book and in 1942 there appeared *Counseling and Psychotherapy: Newer Concepts in Practice*. It was in this book that the term 'client' first appeared and also the first complete published transcript of a course of therapy. The technological complexity which lay behind the accomplishment of the latter can be guessed at when it is remembered that at that time two recording machines were used containing 78 r.p.m. discs which had to be changed every three minutes.

The reaction to this second book was in many respects similar to that provoked by the Minnesota lecture. There were those who found it immensely attractive, and many graduate students at Ohio State often referred to it as 'The Bible'. On the larger psychological community, however, it seemed to make little impact and it was not, in fact, reviewed by any major professional journal. Rogers himself believed that the book was particularly threatening to those practitioners who found it difficult to accept that their clients might know more about their own inner psychological selves than their therapists did with all their professional experience and expertise. This was perhaps the first major example of the unacceptability of client-centred therapy to those who rely heavily upon their own expertise and professional status for a sense of self-worth. The history of the approach is liberally populated by hostile critics of this kind.

Rogers was to remain at Ohio State for only four years. During this brief period his reputation was greatly enhanced for he became known as a person of boundless energy with a thirst for innovation and a great love of students. This latter point is of immeasurable importance because it partly explains the extraordinary impact of Rogers' influence in the years ahead. His attitude to students was consistently encouraging and respectful: he treated them as equals and often allowed them to evaluate their own work. The environment for learning which he created enabled them to gain rapidly in confidence and they, in turn, became his greatest supporters and associates. Rogers' undoubted gifts for relating to young people were perhaps instrumental in gaining him his next post. In 1945 he moved to the University of Chicago, having been invited there with the specific request that he should establish a Counseling Center.

The Chicago Years

Rogers spent twelve years at Chicago and certainly considered this period as the most creative part of his career up to that point. The Counseling Center rapidly established itself as an invaluable resource both for the students of the University and for people in the community. Rogers gathered around him a group of highly motivated and innovative colleagues and graduate students and, once more, created a context in which each individual could develop and flourish. The University administration had difficulty with his refusal to 'lead' the Center in the conventional way. True to his principles, he believed in the capacity of the group to find its own way forward and by refusing to exert his authority in the normal way he helped establish a truly democratic climate in which power-sharing became a daily reality. The years did not pass without difficulty, however, for democratic government does not necessarily result in unity or cohesiveness. There were often sharp conflicts and disagreements but Rogers did nothing to dampen these down: instead the open expression of feelings was encouraged and in this way the staff of the Center came to recognize that they were participating in an enterprise where they could exert influence and where their voices would not be ignored. Research flourished as never before and clinical innovations abounded. Rogers was deeply involved in therapeutic work and for two years at Chicago he underwent a period of great personal distress largely induced by a particularly demanding and highly disturbed female client. The personal crisis which resulted from this relationship threatened to undermine him completely and he later commented that it was fortunate for him that by this time he had trained therapists sufficiently well to enable him to receive the kind of help that he himself desperately needed. He emerged from this dark period able to accept himself and to give and receive love in a way which had not previously been possible. It was as if the originator of client-centred therapy had finally achieved the state of being which his work had made possible for countless clients before him. It is not, perhaps, too fanciful to suggest that Carl Rogers was led to create client-centred therapy because he himself so badly needed the kind of healing it offered.

In 1951 Rogers' third major book, *Client-Centered Therapy*, appeared and immediately won a large and enthusiastic readership despite, again, the coolness of the psychological press. In many ways the book is a review of the activities of the Counseling

Center. It explores the application of the client-centred approach not only to individual therapy but to play therapy, groupwork, leadership and administrative roles and to teaching and training. In his own eyes, however, the crowning point of Rogers' achievement to this point was the presentation to him in 1956 by the American Psychological Association of the Distinguished Scientific Contribution Award. Rogers saw this not only as a tangible reward for the numerous research studies which he and his colleagues had conducted into therapeutic process but also as a clear sign that his fellow psychologists were not simply embarrassed by him but were actually to some extent admiring of his work. He later commented that of all the honours he was to receive, this award in 1956 had the greatest personal meaning (Kirschenbaum, 1979: 222).

The award had been preceded in 1954 by the publication of *Psychotherapy and Personality Change*, which Rogers edited with Rosalind Dymond. This book consisted of a number of studies which were, on the whole, supportive of client-centred hypotheses and the psychology journals at last reacted favourably. There can be little doubt that Rogers' research endeavours during this period were to have a profound effect on the whole field of counselling and psychotherapy in the years ahead. From this time onwards it would become increasingly difficult for therapists to evade the stern test of research investigation. As in so many other areas, Rogers was largely responsible for stripping away the mystique from therapeutic relationships and making them accessible not only to scientific researchers but also to ordinary members of the public who might themselves want to consult a therapist one day. Understandably, this kind of activity did not endear Rogers to those who preferred to maintain the veil of secrecy and to hide behind complex theories of human personality. When, in 1957, Rogers felt confident enough to develop what he called 'The necessary and sufficient conditions of therapeutic personality change' he did so against the background not only of vast experience but also of the most rigorous research known in the psychotherapeutic field up to that time (Rogers, 1957a). This, too, did not make him popular with those who had never conducted a research study in their lives and who continued to protest that so delicate a matter as a therapeutic relationship could never be explored adequately through such scientific methodology.

It is intriguing to speculate on what would have happened if Rogers had stayed at Chicago until his retirement. It is conceivable that many benefits would have accrued and that the future of client-centred therapy might have been well served. Certainly Rogers was never again to work with so stimulating and dedicated a group of colleagues and when, somewhat suddenly, he announced his intention of leaving in 1957 in order to take up a post at his old University, Wisconsin, there was almost universal dismay. Interestingly enough, Rogers felt sufficiently uncomfortable about the move to write a lengthy letter to the staff in an attempt to explain his decision (Kirschenbaum, 1979: 243–4).

This letter gives a fascinating insight into his personality and merits close analysis. By far the most important reason for the move, it seems, was Rogers' belief that his new post would give him the chance to make much 'greater impact'. The letter makes it clear that Rogers was much concerned to be influential in the whole field of mental health and saw himself as having important theories to convey. It is not going too far, I believe, to detect in him a crusading spirit which saw in the Wisconsin post an irresistible opportunity for spreading the message. The evangelical tradition of his childhood was still coursing in his veins, even if the cause was now somewhat changed. The particular attraction of Wisconsin was that Rogers would have the chance to work in both the departments of psychology and psychiatry. He had a vision of trainee psychologists and psychiatrists sitting in the same seminar and participating in the same research projects with him. The letter to his bewildered Chicago colleagues waxes lyrical on this aspect and goes so far as to suggest that he would also have the chance 'to influence the University in more general ways'. Almost shamefacedly he acknowledges the attraction of living 'in a beautiful spot', but this is dismissed as of minor importance compared to making 'a significant dent in a new situation during thirteen to fifteen years before I retire'. A most revealing postscript portrays Rogers as 'kin to the old frontiersmen', already half-way to the new location and keen to leave his old haunts behind him. He describes himself as the adventurer who thirsts for new terrain to conquer and new problems to overcome. It seems hardly likely that the Chicago team would have gained much comfort from the letter however much Rogers protested that his new plans in no way altered his affection for them. There must have been many who saw Rogers, perhaps for the first time, as a man of driving ambition who was determined to be influential even if this meant leaving his friends and disappointing those who had relied on his support.

Disillusion in Wisconsin

The move to Wisconsin was in many ways a disaster. Rogers' vision of psychology and psychiatry holding hands was never fulfilled and he was quickly at loggerheads with many of his new colleagues, especially in the Psychology Department where a rule of veiled terror predominated so that graduate students were kept in place by a succession of examinations and the fear of failure. So great were the conflicts that in the end Rogers resigned from the department, although he continued to work with the Psychiatric Institute.

The Wisconsin years did, however, lead to one major research project. For some time Rogers had been keen to see if his hypothesis about the necessary and sufficient conditions of personality change would work with seriously disturbed people, and his position within the Department of Psychiatry provided the ideal opportunity to put this to the test. A project of great complexity was set up involving a large number of research workers to whom, in his usual style, Rogers delegated much responsibility and autonomy. The resulting process was far from satisfactory and there were many difficulties and conflicts. Rogers was later to describe the project as 'without doubt the most painful and anguished episode of my whole professional life' (in Burton, 1972: 62). Nor were the results of the study particularly exciting. There were no significant differences between the therapy group and the control group although high therapeutic conditions of congruence and empathy *did* correlate with client improvement. In brief, the project provided some solid support for Rogers' principal theories but the overall findings were modest in their persuasiveness.

It could justifiably be claimed that the powerful desire to be more influential which took Rogers to Wisconsin was in no way fulfilled by the daily work he did there. Yet it was his fifth book, *On Becoming a Person*, published in 1961 that, almost overnight, catapulted him into the limelight and brought him more fame and influence than he could ever have hoped for. The book broke free from the professional world of psychology and showed that client-centred principles had application in almost every facet of day-to-day living. The book does not draw particularly on Rogers' experiences at Wisconsin but is an expression of his thought and feeling in such powerful and moving language that it established him as a communicator of the highest order. Educators, therapists, philosophers, scientists, artists and countless 'men and women in the street' were drawn to the book in their thousands and Rogers was overwhelmed by appreciative letters from persons in almost every walk of life. He went to Wisconsin to make an impact, and he notably failed. He wrote a book and discovered that he was suddenly influential beyond his wildest dreams. In 1963 he announced his decision to resign from the University. He no longer had need of the conventional academic environment and was finding it increasingly restrictive and alienating. The extraordinary success of *On Becoming a Person* gave him the confidence to set out on an altogether more risky path and to forego the security of established institutions. When Richard Farson, one of his former students, invited him in the summer of 1963 to join him and others at the recently created Western Behavioral Sciences Institute Rogers was forced to recognize that he was at a professional crossroads. After initial hesitation he accepted and set out for La Jolla in California to join WBSI, a non-profit-making organization concerned chiefly with humanistically orientated research in interpersonal relations. The 'frontiersman' was once more on the trail but this time the new terrain was particularly hazardous. In previous generations members of the Rogers clan might well have set out on such a venture with a bible in their pack. Rogers had the security of his own experience and reputation but it is doubtful if he would have found the courage if he, too, had not had a book in his suitcase. *On Becoming a Person* was at one and the same time both the challenge and the guide which Rogers needed to leave the university system behind him. In writing it for others he had once again provided himself with the resource he required.

The California Years

The Western Behavioral Sciences Institute

Rogers found the freedom from university life enormously exhilarating. He and Helen found a beautiful house with a spectacular view of the Pacific and he immediately settled down to work with enthusiasm in the new environment. Without the constraints of academic institutional life he was free to develop both professionally and personally in ways that startled many of his friends and even members of his own family. Most significantly, he became greatly involved in the encounter group movement and within a year or two of arriving in La Jolla he was already seen throughout America as an elder statesman of the encounter culture. After the period at Wisconsin, with much of its focus on the seriously disturbed, it seemed that Rogers welcomed the opportunity to work with a more 'normal' population. He began to trust the wisdom of the small group with the same confidence that he had previously shown towards individual clients. At the same time he found it possible to use the group context for his own development and he became markedly more expressive of his own feelings and more prepared to risk being vulnerable in relationships. These changes in his own behaviour were accompanied by an increasing fascination with the application of client-centred principles in settings outside the therapy room. When, in 1970, *Carl Rogers on Encounter Groups* appeared it sold more than a quarter of a million copies and this followed on *Freedom to Learn: A View of What Education Might Become*, which was first published in 1969 and eventually sold more than 300,000 copies. Rogers was now a 'big name' and it seemed that the more he realized his ambition to become widely influential the more it was possible for him to extend the area of personal freedom and to be open and responsive to others in new ways and at a deeper level.

The Center for Studies of the Person
In 1968 Richard Farson left WBSI to take up a new position and this seems to have brought about changes in the administrative policy of the Institute which Rogers found uncongenial. He did not waste time fighting the changes but instead joined with others in the organization to form the Center for Studies of the Person, which still exists and of which Rogers remained a 'Resident Fellow' (his own chosen title) until his death. The Center soon had about forty members drawn from different disciplines and its affairs were conducted in such a way that each member was free to develop his or her own interests within the supportive environment of like-minded people, all of whom were deeply interested in persons and in the essential value of subjective experience. From this base Rogers was to continue an active professional life for a further twenty years and there is no doubt that, despite difficulties and conflicts, CSP provided him with a rich network of companionship and stimulus which enabled him to enjoy a particularly productive and energetic old age.

The Global Community

During this final period Rogers only spasmodically returned to the issues and challenges of individual therapy although he was frequently happy to demonstrate his approach on film or to carry out therapeutic interviews during workshops and conferences. Increasingly, however, his interest was drawn to the concerns of everyday life and to the problems confronting the global community. *Becoming Partners*, published in 1972, was an attempt to explore the institution of marriage and its alternatives, and in 1977 he wrote *Carl Rogers on Personal Power* in which he gave expression to the political implications of his ideas for many aspects of life from the family to the wider arenas of education, business and national life. During this period, too, often with the help of his daughter, Natalie, Rogers initiated a series of large group workshops where it was possible to apply the approach to groups of between 75 and 800 people. It was in the mid-1970s that Rogers first coined the expression 'person-centred' to describe these residential events and he increasingly employed this term when his approach was utilized in settings other than that of counselling and psychotherapy.

Perhaps it was inevitable that his involvement first in small group work and then with large groups should eventually lead Rogers to consider the application of his approach to issues facing the world community. In the final years of his life he was much preoccupied with world peace and with the crossing of cultural and racial boundaries. In his seventies and eighties he continued to display astonishing vitality and travelled the world in order to make his ideas known, especially in those areas where tension and conflict were day-to-day realities. Northern Ireland, South Africa, Poland and Russia amongst others featured on his itinerary in these years and in each country he not only talked about his work but actively participated in workshops and seminars so that people in these countries could experience, however briefly, what it might mean to respond to each other in a person-centred way. His book, *A Way of Being*, published in 1980, contains amongst other papers on his changing views a powerful vision of the possible world of tomorrow. Towards the end of 1985 he fulfilled his cherished ambition of bringing together influential leaders of seventeen different countries in a residential conference on the 'Central American Challenge', which was held in Austria. This conference was the most outstanding example of his utter commitment in the final years of his life to the preservation of world peace and to the avoidance of nuclear conflict. It was entirely fitting that when Rogers died on 4 February 1987, after a fall, he had, unbeknown to him, just been nominated for the Nobel Peace Prize.

The Spiritual Dimension

This introductory exploration of Rogers' life and work would be incomplete without one further discussion. It would seem that the young man who had set out to become a farmer and had then changed direction to become a Christian minister had moved a long way from his initial moorings by the time of his death as the world-renowned psychologist, therapist and peace worker. Yet I am tempted to believe that this was not altogether the case and that the clue to the essential continuity in his development as a person lies in the hiddenness of his spiritual pilgrimage. It is to this that I wish now to turn.

There can be no doubt that the young Rogers was a deeply religious man. His letters and diary entries in the period prior to and during the China trip show a certain theological turmoil but this is always allied to a powerful idealism and, increasingly, to a deep admiration for and attraction to the personality of Christ. Equally there is no doubt that once Rogers had made the decision to abandon his training for the Christian ministry he turned his back not only on the Christian church but on any overt belief in the Christian religion.

I have attempted to show elsewhere (Thorne, 1990) that this complete rejection of his Christian past can be explained, at least to some extent, by the perverse theology of the fundamentalistic evangelicalism of his childhood. Rogers' experience as a therapist and psychologist brought him increasingly to the conviction that human beings are essentially forward-moving organisms drawn to the fulfilment of their own creative natures and to the pursuit of truth and social responsiveness. Such a conviction stood in sharp contrast to the negative and guilt-inducing view of human nature enshrined in the severe interpretation of the doctrine of Original Sin which characterized the theology of the Rogers' household. Within this perspective only the redeeming 'blood of the Lamb' could wipe away the foulness of sin and hold out for men and women the possibility of salvation. Without such an operation, demanding repentance and conversion, there could be little hope for an essentially corrupt and fallen human race. Such a view became increasingly unacceptable and distasteful to Rogers, for it ran counter to his experience as a therapist and to his understanding of the evolutionary processes in the created order. As a psychologist and as a scientist he found the concepts of sinfulness and fallenness with their inherent judgementalism, repugnant and ultimately life-denying and deeply injurious to the human spirit.

The inner perturbation and 'breakdown' during the Chicago years indicate that at the deepest level Rogers was by no means free of the insidious conditioning of his childhood and adolescence. During his own therapy after the near catastrophe with his psychotic female client he was brought face to face with the extent of his self-rejection and with the deep-seated belief in his own unworthiness. Once released from the grip of these convictions he was able to experience the self-acceptance and the deep capacity for intimacy that his own work had already made possible for countless clients. In the light of the deep wounds to his own psyche which were revealed at this time Rogers turned his back with apparent finality on the Christian faith and on every aspect of institutionalized religion. So deep were these wounds and so gradual the recovery that it was only in the final years of his life that Rogers was able once more to approach the world of spiritual reality. The death of his wife, Helen, in 1979 was the occasion for a resurgence of his interest in the invisible world and for a while he became immersed in the mysterious implications of psychic phenomena. It was at this time, too, that he began again to consider the possibility of some kind of life beyond death and to deepen his interest in certain aspects of eastern religious experience.

In the final period of his life, however, it was in the therapeutic relationship itself that Rogers rediscovered the dimension which at a conscious level he had shut out when he abandoned Christianity. In the last description he published of a therapeutic encounter he was able to write: 'I realize that this account partakes of the mystical. Our experiences, it is clear, involve the transcendent, the indescribable, the spiritual. I am impelled to believe that I, like many others, have underestimated the importance of this mystical, spiritual dimension' (Rogers, 1986b: 200). It appears that once again, and for the final time, Rogers the therapist had discovered the truth of which Rogers the man had greatest need. He viewed the prospect of death with equanimity while celebrating life by entering into love relationships with women which gave him intense pleasure and enrichment. For him the spiritual dimension of these final years was linked to an increasing capacity for intimacy and mutuality.

In many ways the milestones along the path of Rogers' often hidden spiritual pilgrimage can be seen in an interview given in 1990 by Elizabeth Sheerer, one of the original members of the Counseling Center at the University of Chicago. Her interviewer, Phillip Barrineau, asks towards the end of their conversation:

> You've noted that the [person-centred] approach has gone into so many areas; are there areas or issues that have not been addressed in your estimation?

Elizabeth Sheerer's reply is exceptionally revealing:

> Yes, I would like more attention to the spiritual part of the person. . . . Of course, it's not missing in client-centered therapy but it's not addressed formally. It's not recognised formally. You don't get into therapy without getting in touch with the spiritual aspect of the person. *Phillip Barrineau*: Do you have a theory about why it's not addressed formally?
> *Elizabeth Sheerer*: Yes, I do. That's Carl. This was an area of difficulty for Carl. We learned early in the game not to talk about religion with

Carl. That was a taboo subject because it was uncomfortable for him. . . . I always had a notion that something happened while he was in China, that never was spoken of publicly or in print . . . in the years that he was developing the theory, he just didn't want any part of formal religion or, as far as I could tell, any religion. But of course, his work is so profoundly influenced by his background in Christianity. I don't think he could have developed without that background. (Barrineau, 1990: 423–4)

2

Rogers' Major Theoretical Contributions

Theory from Experience

Rogers tended to be highly suspicious of theories. His early experience of theological doctrine and later of psychoanalytical and behaviouristic dogma led him to the conclusion that the premature application of theoretical models made it more difficult to trust the evidence of one's own perceptions and intuitions. Most importantly, he discovered in his early clinical work that a reliance on theory could lead to a situation where the therapist attempted to fit or mould a client into a preconceived cognitive structure rather than engaging with the client's world as he or she experienced it. There came a time, as we have seen, when Rogers dared to view himself as a pioneer who could legitimately lay aside previous theories, however elegantly and persuasively expressed, and devote his energy instead to relating deeply to his clients and discovering with them what worked.

In this decision to liberate himself from the constraints of previous theories and to trust the empirical validity of his own experience Rogers was already establishing a baseline of cardinal importance. In this he was encouraged by his understanding of the work of John Dewey and his followers and by the influence of Otto Rank as it was channelled to him through Jessie Taft and her colleagues. Essentially Rogers came to believe that what mattered was not some concept of objective reality, whatever that might be, but the way in which a given person perceives reality. In brief, the surest route to understanding a person's behaviour is to come to a knowledge of that person's subjective awareness of himself or herself and of the world in which he or she exists. Such an approach takes as its basic assumption that a person's subjective experience is worthy of the deepest respect even if to others it may appear bizarre or misguided. For Rogers the trusting of his own experience was therefore paralleled by his commitment to trusting the experience of his client. Any theory or therapeutic procedure that threatened to undermine this trust either in himself or in his client became for Rogers an impediment to the therapeutic process and potentially destructive of a healthy therapeutic relationship.

The revolutionary nature of this point of view may not initially be apparent but it is clear that, at a stroke, it throws into question the notion of the therapist as an expert with special knowledge. For Rogers the expert role implied a relationship where the therapist is perceived as an authority figure and this immediately engendered a power imbalance. The issue of power is central to his understanding of the therapeutic relationship and during his Rochester days Rogers concluded that the therapist's theoretical knowledge could lead him to suppose that he actually knew more about the client's inner functioning than the client did. Once such a dangerous fantasy was established it became difficult, if not impossible, for the client to put trust in his or her own experiencing and in the validity of his or her own perceptions. And yet without such trust the client's subjective world would be unlikely to assume the supreme importance it merited in the therapeutic enterprise.

In his insistence on the centrality of subjective experience Rogers is in the mainstream of the phenomenological tradition, which holds to the belief that each of us behaves in accordance with our subjective awareness of ourselves and of the world we inhabit. Rogers' importance lies in his single-minded application of this belief to the task of therapy. In his clinical practice he increasingly became convinced that it is always the client who knows what hurts and in what direction he or she needs to proceed if healing is to take place. The therapist's function is to aid the client in the exploration and discovery of his or her own inner resources: it is not to impose, however gently, external solutions, strategies, interpretations or explanations.

It is clear that the confidence Rogers placed in a person's 'inner resources' could only spring from a basically optimistic view of human nature. In this optimism Rogers was again supported by the 'progressive' educators such as John Dewey and his disciple, William Heard Kilpatrick, who believed essentially that children knew what they needed to learn and how best to acquire the necessary knowledge. Such optimism stands in stark contrast, for example, to the view of Freud, who tended to be pessimistic about human nature and had grave doubts about the future of mankind. It is also contrary to the view that Rogers would have received through the brand of evangelical Christianity embraced by his family, although, interestingly, at Union he would have been influenced by other theological opinions which differed markedly from the 'totally corrupt' school of thought favoured in the Rogers household.

For Rogers the trust in subjective experience and the belief in the essential truthworthiness of human nature went hand in hand. He discovered in the early years of his clinical practice that when he was able to commit himself to a deep understanding of his client's subjective world and was perceived as doing so by the client, then almost invariably the client would begin to behave in ways which were positive and forward moving. It is not too simplistic to affirm that the whole conceptual framework of Rogers' ideas rests on his profound experience that human beings become increasingly trustworthy once they feel at a deep level that their subjective experience is both respected and progressively understood. Throughout five decades of professional work he did not deviate from this belief but, on the contrary, discovered more and more evidence to support it. It is to the development and elaboration of this basic conviction that we now turn. Throughout the rest of this chapter the corpus of Rogers' theoretical formulations will be treated as a total body of knowledge, although clearly such formulations developed and evolved over time and in practice certain dimensions received more focused attention at one time than at another.

The Actualizing Tendency

Rogers came to believe that there is only one single, basic human motive and to this he gave the name 'the actualizing tendency'. In common with the rest of the created order the human being, in Rogers' understanding, has an underlying and inherent tendency both to maintain itself and to move towards the constructive accomplishment of its potential. Just as a tulip instinctively moves towards becoming as complete and perfect a tulip as possible, so the human being moves towards growth and fulfilment and the accomplishment of the highest possible level of 'human-beingness'. The only constraints placed upon the actualizing tendency arise from the environment in which the person finds himself or herself. Just as the tulip is unlikely to flourish in poor soil and without proper care and watering, so, too, the growth of the human being will be stunted if the conditions for the encouragement of the actualizing tendency are unfavourable.

When we remember Rogers' adolescent years and his background in agricultural science it may not seem surprising that he was attracted to the simplicity of a principle which appears to have general validity throughout the natural order. The actualizing tendency, however, does not perhaps do full justice to the uniqueness of the human person and Rogers was always at pains to point out that the specifics of human growth can and do vary widely from person to person. Actualization involves the differentiation of organs and functions and a development towards autonomy: in this way the process of actualization is keenly sensitive to the subtle complexity of human differences.

This basic actualizing tendency is the only motive to appear in the whole of Rogers' theoretical system. It is clear that it is only the *organism as a whole* which manifests this tendency and that Rogers was acutely aware that *parts* of the organism – particularly those concerned with self-perception – could fundamentally inhibit or distort the general tendency of the total organism. Actualization includes such motivational drives as need-reduction or tension-reduction and also incorporates what might be termed 'growth motivations' such as the seeking of creative challenges or the desire to learn, even if painful effort is involved. In his final exposition of client-centred therapy (Rogers and Sanford, 1989) Rogers openly acknowledged that the actualizing tendency is in no way unique to his own theoretical viewpoint. He notes that the concept runs through all of Maslow's writings and is reflected in the work of biologists such as Szent-Gyorgyi, who concludes that there is definitely a drive to perfection in all living matter. In this final paper, too, Rogers is clear that the hindrance to actualization can come from sub-parts of the human organism which have themselves been adversely affected by a whole range of environmental circumstances, both physical and psychological. He states that the actualizing tendency can even be stunted or stopped altogether. Sometimes, too, it is only able to exert itself in 'warped, bizarre or abnormal manifestations; and turns in socially destructive ways rather than constructive ways' (Rogers and Sanford, 1989: 1492).

The concept of the human organism as a unity and the belief that it is this unity which demonstrates the tendency to actualization are crucial to Rogers' understanding of the self and of the way in which the development of the self can serve the actualizing tendency or impede it. If the experience of the self and the total experience of the organism are relatively harmonious, then the actualizing tendency remains tolerably unified. If, however, self and organismic experience are discordant then the actualizing tendency will be frustrated to perhaps a damaging degree. For Rogers the tendency to actualize the self is essentially a 'subsystem' of the actualizing tendency and one which can become seriously at cross purposes with the inherent drive of the organism as a whole. It is to this 'subsystem' with its crucial significance for a human being's development that we now turn.

Self-actualization and the Concept of Self
In 1959 Rogers published a lengthy and detailed exposition of his theoretical position of which he was inordinately proud and which subsequently received little of the attention it undoubtedly merited (Rogers, 1959). The reasons for this neglect are difficult to understand for the article, which runs to seventy-two pages, throws immense light not only on all the major theoretical constructs but also on the history of their development. Indeed, when he came to discuss the concept of the self Rogers felt it appropriate to insert a 'digression on the case history of a construct' and these few pages provide a striking example of the process through which many of his central theories gradually took shape. He sums this up as 'clinical observation, initial conceptualization, initial crude research to test some of the hypotheses involved, further clinical observation, more rigorous formulation of the construct and its functional relationships, more refined operational definitions of the construct, more conclusive research' (Rogers, 1959: 203). It is difficult to imagine a way of working which could more clearly reflect the refusal to formulate theory until it had been through the repeated and painstaking tests of clinical experience, cognitive reflection and scientific research.

Rogers opens his digression by admitting that he began his professional work with the conviction that the self was a useless and meaningless term which had no place in the psychologist's vocabulary. As always, however, he subjected this conviction to the test of clinical experience and gradually discovered that, once clients were given the opportunity to express their concerns in their own words without interference from the therapist, they almost invariably tended to talk in terms of the self. There was often a profound dissatisfaction at their inability to give adequate expression to the self, or with their current evaluation of the self. They were apt to make remarks such as: 'I feel I'm not being my real self', 'I wonder who I really am', 'It feels good to just be myself here', 'I don't want anyone to know the real me'. Such statements obviously indicated that the self was a significant element in the client's experience and often a perplexing and distressing one. Furthermore, there often seemed to be an implied goal which was connected with the evolution of a 'real' self or the aspiration to an 'ideal' self. For many clients both states of being seemed equally impossible of attainment.

In clinical practice another aspect became apparent. It seemed that the concept of the self was subject to wild fluctuation and that the process of therapy had a not inconsiderable bearing on these fluctuations. It was not unusual for a client to experience himself during therapy in a fairly positive light and to feel an increasing confidence in the ability to tackle the problems with which life was confronting him. A few days later, however, he might well return to the therapist with his self-concept changed beyond all recognition and with feelings of worthlessness or immaturity in the ascendant. Rogers concluded from these changes and modifications in the self-concept that the self is not a fixed entity but a product of the person's response to experience which takes the form of a 'conceptual gestalt composed of perceptions of the characteristics of the "I" or "me" and the perceptions of the relationships of the "I" or "me" to others and to various aspects of life, together with the values attached to these perceptions' (Rogers, 1959: 200). Additionally, the 'gestalt' is fluid and changing but is nevertheless a specific entity at any given moment which can to some extent be defined in operational terms. More simply put, I am the self which I currently conceptualize myself as being. This conceptualization, however, is dependent not only on thousands of experiences and conditionings which constitute my past but also on the unpredictable events and interactions which may occur at any moment. It is possible for me to experience my 'self' as happy, confident and assured at one moment and despairing, inadequate and demoralized the next. Yet the event which may have brought about this startling transformation may be nothing more than the powerful comment of a fellow human being. In such an unreliable context as human existence it is scarcely surprising that for many people the process of self-actualization is fraught with complexity and anxiety. Small wonder, too, that so hazardous and unpredictable a process frequently finds itself at variance with the actualizing tendency of the organism as a whole. For those people who find their way to the therapist's door this clash between the struggle for self-actualization and the basic tendency of the human organism may well have reached a point of intolerable tension. The question which now arises is why for some people the striving for self-actualization should lead to such alienation from their organismic integrity.

Conditions of Worth

Rogers' optimistic view of human nature is reflected in his postulated characteristics of the human infant. He sees the individual during the period of early infancy as having an inherent tendency towards actualizing his or her organism and as perceiving his or her experience as reality. There is therefore no conflict between the interaction with reality and the basic actualizing tendency. Indeed the two may be seen as harmoniously interactive, for the infant also engages in an organismic valuing process which has as its referent the actualizing tendency. In this way the infant has no difficulty in establishing which experiences are good for the organism and which are bad. The infant accordingly embraces positively valued experiences and avoids those which are negative and potentially damaging to the organism. Briefly put, the infant has both an inherent motivational system and a regulating system through the valuing process which ensures that the organism gets what it needs for its satisfaction.

The trouble begins, and for some it can be big trouble, when the actualizing tendency leads towards the differentiation that results in a part of the individual's experience becoming symbolized in an awareness of being. In other words, the infant begins to experience himself or herself as a self different and separate from other selves. Gradually, principally through relationship with significant others, the infant comes to have a concept of self which in its turn requires nurturing and protecting.

As the awareness, or consciousness, of self develops a new need emerges which is of extreme potency. This need was first formulated in 1954 by Rogers' associate, Standal, who defined it as the *need for positive regard* (Standal, 1954). Standal believed it to be a learned need but whether this is so or not is largely irrelevant for it appears to be universal and, in Rogers' words, 'pervasive and persistent' (Rogers, 1959: 223). The strength of this need cannot, in Rogers' view, be overestimated and its satisfaction quickly becomes of overriding concern for the developing child. Indeed, the need is so great that its satisfaction becomes more vital than experiences which favour the actualizing of the total organism. The fortunate child is the one whose need for positive regard is readily and consistently satisfied by the significant others in his or her life and who is not constantly having to 'ignore' organismic needs in the desperate search for positive regard.

Allied to the need for positive regard there develops over time the need for self-regard. We require at some level and in some way, however minimal, to feel good about ourselves and if this need is not met it is difficult to function in the world. Sadly, as Rogers and his colleagues discovered, those persons who have received only highly selective positive regard from significant others are hard pressed to maintain self-regard to any degree at all. The infant who is surrounded by critical and disapproving people or by those who constantly give ambiguous or conflicting signals becomes painfully confused. He or she is permanently anxious and is forever seeking ways of discovering how to win at least the occasional sign of love or affection. It is likely that some areas of potential validation will be discovered and the individual may learn how to develop behaviours which earn a limited approval. It may be, for example, that a girl discovers that she can win parental favour if she reads books, never loses her temper and keeps her clothes spotlessly clean. Within this highly circumscribed framework she may win some positive regard, but the likelihood of this being converted into anything more than a fragile and precarious self-regard is slim especially if she knows that often she hates reading, feels violently angry inside and longs to roll in the mud. Our capacity to feel positive about ourselves is dependent upon the quality and consistency of the positive regard shown to us by others, and where this has been selective (as to some degree it must be for all of us) we are the victims of what Rogers described as *conditions of worth*. In other words, our self-regard becomes as selective if not more so than the regard bestowed on us by others. We have worth in our own eyes only on condition that we think, feel and behave in ways that others have told us are worthy of love and respect. For many people this whole sad process leads to an introjection of values which emanate from judgemental and punitive parents or other significant figures and bear little or no relationship to the needs of the human organism for actualization. On the contrary, the painful and bewildering quest for positive regard, where so little is to be found, results in a human being who is crippled by a sense of personal worthlessness (a total lack of self-regard) and who is utterly divorced from his or her organismic roots and the valuing process with which he or she was in contact before the consciousness of self emerged. The constant introjection of alien values has resulted in the internalization of conditions of worth, which makes authentic living well-nigh impossible.

As a result of the overwhelming need for positive regard it is evident that for many people there develops over time a marked discrepancy between the self as perceived and the actual experience of the total organism. Where such a discrepancy exists Rogers speaks of an incongruence between self and experience. This incongruence leads to a psychological vulnerability which will often render the person anxious and confused whenever an experience is perceived or in some way anticipated as being incongruent with the structure of the self and the current self-concept. The outcome of psychological vulnerability of this kind is a defensive response to experiences that in some way threaten the person's concept of self. The defensive behaviour can take a number of forms but, for Rogers, the responses of distortion or denial are perhaps the most common. It might be, for example that a child in its search for positive regard has introjected a whole range of beliefs, judgements and attitudes (principally from the parents) many of which may run quite counter to its own organismic response to experience. The child is subject to many conditions of worth in so far as its experience of approval from the parents is conditional upon certain behaviours. In this situation a self-concept gradually takes shape which is aligned with the parental view of what is acceptable and admirable. The person may come to view himself or herself as, for example, patient, logical, calm and unprejudiced because such qualities are highly valued by the parents. Such a self-concept may win approval and render life tolerable but the person's self-regard will be dependent upon its maintenance. On those occasions when he or she senses the presence of inner feelings of intolerance or agitation the self-concept will be threatened. The defence of distortion comes into play if the person in such a situation attempts to view reality so that the threatening feelings can be dismissed as the outcome, for example, of holding too high principles or as an appropriate response to outrageous behaviour by another person. Denial takes place when the person utterly rejects even the possibility of intolerance or agitation in himself or herself while to everyone else they are plain to see in words or behaviour. Where the self-concept is hedged around with so many conditions of worth that distortion or denial of this kind are brought into play there is clearly a measure of psychological disturbance present within the person. It is equally evident, however, that the disturbed person may have little or no awareness of the disturbance. Nor need he or she necessarily be perceived as disturbed by others for they, too, may have a vested interest in maintaining or even encouraging what is, in effect, a tragic but rigorous act of self-deception.

Locus of Evaluation

Those persons who in their search for positive regard have been forced to internalize numerous conditions of worth will have little faith in their own judgement. Furthermore, whatever face they succeed in showing to the world, they are likely to hold themselves in low esteem and to have no confidence in their capacity to make appropriate decisions or to choose satisfactory courses of action. In Rogers' terminology they will lack an internalized locus of evaluation. This somewhat inelegant term is used to indicate the source of evidence about values and meaning. The individual who has lost touch with the actualizing tendency because of distorted self-actualization will no longer be at the centre of the valuing process.

He or she will not be able to trust the evidence being supplied by his or her own senses and instead will constantly refer to the judgement of others in order to establish the value of an object or experience.

In many ways the level of dependence on an external locus of evaluation is a reliable criterion for determining the presence of psychological disturbance. Disturbed people constantly betray the lack of an internal locus and turn desperately to external authorities or find themselves trapped in a paralysis of indecision. Briefly summarized, Rogers conceptualized disturbance as a greater or lesser degree of alienation from the total organism prompted by the inadequate satisfaction of the fundamental need for positive regard from others and for the self-regard which is dependent on it. Those who are unlucky enough to be brought up amongst a number of significant others who are highly censorious or parsimonious in their approval will develop self-concepts that are usually negative and always falsely based, and will have little prospect of maintaining and nurturing the internal locus of evaluation of which they have need if they are to become autonomous persons in their own right.

The Fully Functioning Person

Rogers has sometimes been accused of neglecting personality theory and offering only a hazy view of human development. Such an accusation is misplaced. On the contrary, his theory, based solidly on clinical experience, is explicit and forceful. As so often with Rogers' formulations, the theory is relatively uncomplicated and rigorously avoids hypotheses which are by definition untestable because of their reliance on concepts of unconscious processes. The theory of personality which he presents is the outcome of his unswerving conviction that, given the right psychological conditions, the individual will discover both how and why he hurts. This discovery will bring with it an understanding of what it means to be truly human and how best to tap and cherish the resources both in the self and in others which can lead to functioning at the highest level. Indeed, Rogers believed that he often witnessed in his clients a movement towards a new way of being and that this closely mirrored the behaviour of psychologically healthy persons who have been fortunate enough to live in contexts that have facilitated the emergence of self-concepts which allow them to be in touch for at least part of the time with their deepest experiences and feelings. Such people demonstrate, as Rogers saw it, what it means to exhibit mature behaviour, a concept he defined in 1959 as the capacity to perceive realistically, to accept responsibility for one's own behaviour, to evaluate experience in terms of the evidence coming from one's own senses, to change the evaluation of experience only on the basis of new evidence, to accept others as unique individuals different from oneself, to prize oneself and to prize others (Rogers, 1959: 207). Rogers further developed this concept of maturity into his view of the fully functioning person, and although such a person may constitute an unattainable ideal Rogers gathered the material for such a vision of human functioning, not from a romanticized Utopia but, as always, from his experience as a therapist. As he himself wrote: 'These views . . . have an empirical or experiential foundation. I have learned what the good life seems to be by observing and participating in the struggle of disturbed and troubled people to achieve that life' (Rogers, 1961: 184).

The first and most striking characteristic of the 'fully functioning person' as Rogers describes him or her is an increasing openness to experience. Such individuals are able to listen to themselves and to others and to allow themselves to experience what is happening without feeling threatened. Secondly, they have an ability to live fully in the present and to be attentive to each moment as it is lived. In this way they demonstrate a preparedness to trust experience rather than fearing it. As a consequence experience becomes the moulding force for the emerging personality rather than having to be twisted or contorted in some way in order to fit a preconceived structure of reality or a heavily defended self-concept. The third characteristic is the organismic trusting which is so notably lacking in those who have constantly fallen victim to the adverse judgement of others. Fully functioning persons regard their organismic experiences, what feels right, as the most valid sources of information for deciding what to do or how to react in any given situation. They are much less inclined to look outside themselves for authoritative guides to behaviour or to defer to others when making decisions. Such organismic trusting is likely to lead to a sense of personal freedom and to a capacity to accept responsibility for determining one's own actions and their consequences. In Rogers' view the mature person experiences himself or herself as having a high degree of autonomy and does not feel imprisoned by fate or circumstances or even by genetic inheritance. There is rather a sense of being a free agent and this often results in a capacity to adjust or adapt to changing conditions and to produce creative ideas or to initiate imaginative projects. Characteristically, fully functioning persons are not trapped in conventional or conformist roles and yet at the same time they relate to society in a way that permits them to be fully involved rather than ostracized because of their apparent eccentricity or anarchic radicalism.

Rogers' view of human development and his concept of the fully functioning person both evolved from clinical practice and it is clear that they belong to a developmental or process theory of human nature. Rogers, in line with many existential thinkers, came to believe that human beings in some measure possess the capacity and have the natural tendency to reorganize and reconstruct their self-concepts in order to make them more congruent with the totality of their experience. Indeed it is this capacity which makes it possible for an individual to move away from a state of psychological maladjustment or disturbance towards a state of psychological adjustment. In the fully elaborated theory of therapy and personality referred to earlier, Rogers defined in precise terms what he understood by these concepts. Psychological maladjustment exists 'when the organism denies to awareness, or distorts in awareness, significant experiences, which consequently are not accurately symbolized or organized into the gestalt of the self-structure, thus creating an incongruence between self and experience'. (Rogers, 1959: 204). Psychological adjustment, on the other hand, exists 'when the concept of the self is such that all experiences are or may be assimilated on a symbolic level into the gestalt of the self-structure. Optimal psychological adjustment is thus synonymous with complete congruence of self and experience, or complete openness to experience' (Rogers, 1959: 206).

It is this movement from the state of maladjustment towards the state of adjustment which Rogers perceived occurring in his therapeutic relationships and he frequently refers to it with a sense of awe. It was the excitement of being involved in what increasingly seemed to him both a miraculous and a predictable process which compelled him to seek an understanding of what it was about the relationship that made such a process possible. The scientist in him needed to know: furthermore it was only through such knowledge that the practice of therapy could move from a largely intuitive undertaking to one of purposeful endeavour. The order of events is significant. Rogers began by trusting his own experience and that of his clients and discovered that such trust initiated and maintained a process whereby the client moved towards a more creative way of being. Only then did the scientific researcher set about discovering the characteristics of this process and determining its essential components. These discoveries were to have a profound influence upon therapy in general and constitute perhaps Rogers' greatest contribution to our understanding of therapeutic relationships.

The Core Conditions

After more research studies than had ever been undertaken previously in the field of psychotherapy, Rogers was able in the detailed statement of 1959 to present his conclusions about the ingredients of the psychologically facilitative climate which promotes therapeutic change. In the posthumous article which he co-authored with Ruth Sanford (Rogers and Sanford, 1989) he remains faithful to the original formulation. It is, in fact, remarkably concise and, as in so many other instances, has earned for Rogers the accusation of naivety and oversimplification.

The first element concerns the client and certainly has about it the ring of the obvious. The client, Rogers maintains, is experiencing at least some level of incongruence which makes him anxious. This apparently self-evident condition presents a crucial criterion for establishing the readiness of the client for therapy. It stresses the necessity of at least some awareness on the client's part of discomfort and of a discrepancy, however minimal, between experience and self-concept. The therapist, by contrast, is congruent in the relationship and experiences harmony between the picture he has of himself, the way he expresses himself and the way he views himself and external reality. Secondly, the therapist embodies and conveys an attitude towards the client which can be described as acceptant and prizing. Thirdly, the therapist achieves an empathic understanding of the client's internal and external reality as if through the client's eyes. Finally, Rogers draws attention to another apparently self-evident condition. He states that it is necessary for the client to perceive, to some minimal degree, the congruence, the acceptance and the understanding of the therapist. In this brief analysis of the psychologically facilitative relationship Rogers, emboldened by practice and research, offers a view of the therapeutic relationship which remains today as radical and disturbing as it did forty years ago. The 'core conditions' of congruence, acceptance and empathy are simple to state, much more difficult to describe and infinitely challenging to practise.

Congruence

Rogers came to believe that congruence or genuineness is the most fundamental of the attitudinal conditions that promote therapeutic growth. Congruence means that the therapist is what he or she is in the relationship without façade and without any attempt to assume or hide behind a professional role. Such congruence, however, is dependent upon the therapist's capacity to maintain a high level of self-awareness. He or she wishes to be constantly in touch with what is being felt at an experiential or visceral (a favourite Rogers word) level and to hold these feelings clearly present in awareness so that they are available for direct communication to the client when this is appropriate. In this sense the therapist is transparent to the client and is able to own, and express if necessary, the thoughts, feelings and attitudes which are currently flowing within him or her. Achieving this condition is no easy task for it requires of the therapist a continuing openness to inner experience even if what is experienced poses a threat to the therapist's self-concept. In effect the therapist is challenged to maintain his or her genuineness by accurately symbolizing and including in the self-concept even those feelings and thoughts which are initially unwelcome and alien. Negative thoughts, feelings and attitudes need particularly to be acknowledged by the therapist and to be held available for expression just as much as positive ones, which can in any case often be inferred from behaviour and tone. Such a stress on realness is strikingly at odds with many of the traditional ideas of the therapeutic relationship and is also liable to frequent misunderstanding. It certainly does not mean that the therapist offloads on to the client all his or her own feelings and concerns; nor does it imply that the therapist impulsively blurts out any passing attitude or intuitive insight. It does mean, however, that the therapist is always at pains to be in touch with his or her own flow of experiencing and does not deny to awareness those aspects of experience which are uncomfortable or disturbing. Congruence demands a willingness to express and to *be*, without inhibition, any persistent feelings that exist in the relationship. It requires at all times that the therapist resist the temptation to seek refuge behind the mask of professionalism, the role of the expert or the mystique of therapeutic process.

Acceptance

The basic need for positive regard which Rogers believed to be universal in human beings and to be pervasive and persistent, has been poorly or rarely met in many persons who present themselves for therapy. It therefore becomes crucially important, in order that the individual may feel acceptance of self, to receive positive regard from the therapist. Rogers' concept of acceptance of which the term 'unconditional positive regard' is an elaboration, implies a caring by the therapist which is totally uncontaminated by judgements or evaluations of the thoughts, feelings or behaviour of the client. The therapist does not accept some aspects of the client and reject others. He or she experiences (and this cannot be simulated) an outgoing, positive, non-possessive warmth for the client. Such acceptance extends to the full range of the client's feelings and attitudes, from hostility and indifference to love and joy. Curiously enough it seems that for some therapists it is more difficult to accept unconditionally a client's positive feelings than his or her negative ones. In his final statement (Rogers and Sanford, 1989), Rogers comments on this strange fact by suggesting that the kind of caring that the person-centred therapist aspires to achieve is a 'gullible' caring. Clients are to be accepted as they say they are and the therapist is to avoid the lurking suspicion that they may be otherwise. Such an attitude, Rogers remarks, is not a sign of the therapist's stupidity but rather the attitude which engenders trust and thus leads to deeper self-exploration and to the correction of false statements. Acceptance of this order is not easily accomplished for it requires of therapists a capacity, from deep within themselves, to accept persons as they are and not as they would wish them to be. Defensive, aggressive, vulnerable and conflicted persons require the healing energy of unconditional positive regard if they are to discover within themselves the enormous potentialities for growth with which they lost contact perhaps in the earliest days of their existence.

Empathy

Rogers wrote extensively about empathy and often suggested that of the three 'core conditions' it is the most trainable. His overriding concern with the client's subjective perceptual world made it imperative that the therapist could achieve as full an understanding as possible of the way in which clients view themselves and the world, for only through such understanding could he or she hope to facilitate the subtle changes in self-concept which make for positive development. Such an understanding involves on the therapist's part a willingness and an ability to enter the private perceptual world of the client without fear and to become thoroughly conversant with it. Rogers wrote of empathy:

> It involves being sensitive, moment to moment, to the changing felt meanings which flow in this other person, to the fear or rage or tenderness or confusion or whatever, that he/she is experiencing. It means temporarily living in his/her life, moving about in it delicately without making judgements, sensing meaning of which he/she is scarcely aware, but not trying to uncover feelings of which the person is totally unaware, since this would be too threatening. It includes communicating your sensings of his/her world as you look with fresh

and unfrightened eyes at elements of which the individual is fearful. It means frequently checking with him/her as to the accuracy of your sensings, and being guided by the responses you receive. You are a confident companion to the person in his/her inner world. (Rogers, 1980: 142)

No therapist can be the 'confident companion' of which Rogers speaks in this moving passage unless he or she is secure enough in his or her own identity to enter the other's world without fear of getting lost in what may turn out to be bizarre or even frightening terrain. There is always what Rogers described as an 'as if' quality about empathy. The therapist enters the client's perceptual world 'as if' it is his or her own but without ever losing the capacity to return to his or her own moorings.

In 1986, shortly before his death, Rogers returned again to the subject of empathy. In an article comparing his use of empathy with that of the psychoanalyst, Heinz Kohut, he expressed his abhorrence of Kohut's apparently cold and impersonal use of empathy as a means of 'collecting information' about the patient's inner life. In contrast he reaffirmed in the strongest possible terms his own conviction that empathy is in itself a powerful healing agent. 'It is one of the most potent aspects of therapy', he wrote, 'because it releases, it confirms, it brings even the most frightened client into the human race. If a person can be understood, he or she belongs' (Rogers, 1986c: 129). It is difficult to imagine a more powerful statement of belief nor is it surprising that Rogers should often lament that so trainable a quality is totally neglected in the professional preparation of many therapists.

A Fourth Condition

It was Rogers' contention – and he held firm to it for over forty years – that if the therapist proves able to offer a facilitative climate where congruence, acceptance and empathy are all present and the client perceives this to be so at some minimal level, then therapeutic movement will occur. For him, the three conditions were not only necessary for effective therapy but also sufficient. In such a climate, he argued, clients will gradually get in touch with their own resources for self-understanding and will prove capable of changing their self-concepts and taking over the direction of their lives. In the posthumous article referred to earlier (Rogers and Sanford, 1989), there is no deviation from this view of the necessary and sufficient conditions for therapeutic movement but, interestingly, the article contains no reference to an earlier article published two years before in which Rogers breaks new ground.

This article, referred to at the end of Chapter 1, acknowledges the existence of a mystical, spiritual dimension (Rogers, 1986b). In the context of this dimension Rogers speaks tentatively of 'one more characteristic' and he does so immediately following a rapid review of the familiar core conditions. There can be no doubt that he viewed this 'characteristic' as in some way of comparable significance to the qualities of congruence, acceptance and empathy. The passage deserves to be quoted in full:

> When I am at my best, as a group facilitator or a therapist, I discover another characteristic. I find that when I am closest to my inner, intuitive self, when I am somehow in touch with the unknown in me, when perhaps I am in a slightly altered state of consciousness in the relationship, then whatever I do seems to be full of healing. Then simply my *presence* is releasing and helpful. There is nothing I can do to force this experience, but when I can relax and be close to the transcendental core of me, then I may behave in strange and impulsive ways in the relationship, ways which I cannot justify rationally, which have nothing to do with my thought processes. But these strange behaviours turn out to be *right*, in some odd way. At those moments it seems that my inner spirit has reached out and touched the inner spirit of the other. Our relationship transcends itself and becomes a part of something larger. Profound growth and healing and energy are present. (Rogers 1986b: 198)

This is a statement which probably did not flow easily from Rogers' pen. In it he speaks of areas of reality to which only a few years previously he would have given little credence. It is perhaps understandable that he refrained from developing further a concept which he was unable to study empirically in the months before his death. I am persuaded, however, that had he lived, we might well have heard much more of the quality of 'presence' of which he speaks in this passage and that both the theory and practice of person-centred therapy might have undergone important revision as a consequence.

The Therapeutic Process

The presence of the core conditions sets in train a directional process which Rogers came to view as predictable and inevitable even if it does not always proceed at the same pace or cover the same psychological distance. Clients, after all, are the judges of the goals or objectives they wish to attain in their process of development and not all will choose to cover the same terrain. For one it may be sufficient to be relieved of intolerable psychological pain while for another the eventual goal may be a level of functioning that far outstrips the original modest expectations which were present at the outset of therapy. Typically, however, when therapy goes well clients will move from a position where their self-concept, usually poor at the entry into therapy and finding expression in behaviour which tends to reinforce the negative evaluation of self, will shift to a position where it more closely approaches the essential worth of the total organism. As the self-concept moves towards a more positive view so, too, clients' behaviour begins to reflect the improvement and to enhance further their perception of themselves.

Rogers was so confident of the potency of the core conditions that he often spoke in 'if . . . then' terms. If the conditions exist, then the process follows. On several occasions he listed examples that typified the stages of the process as he frequently witnessed it in his own clients. His final exposition provides such a list and spells out the changes which are largely implicit in the process. Of critical significance is the client's increasing capacity to be congruent, for it is this change which makes it possible for him or her to be more open to experience and to take in more data more accurately (Rogers and Sanford, 1989: 1493). Congruence, too, leads to the locus of choice being progressively situated within so that the client becomes more confident, self-directing and self-empowered. Perhaps most significantly of all, values are determined by an organismic valuing process that can truly discriminate between positive and negative experiences, those which enhance the organism and those which do it harm. It is experiencing itself which comes to be regarded as a positive, constructive and useful guide even if that experiencing is painful or frustrating. Small wonder that such a trust in experiencing leads to a person who is mature, self-controlled and capable of relating effectively and intimately to others.

Conclusion

Rogers, as we saw earlier, arrived at theoretical formulations only after repeated experience and research studies had persuaded him that they had validity. It is striking that in nearly every instance the theories that emerged are concerned with the monitoring and clarification of processes. Rogers' overriding insistence on the primary importance of being open to experience meant that the kinds of question he pursued were of the 'what' and 'how' rather than the 'why' variety. He was concerned to discover the nature of inner experience and to track wherever possible what was happening within and between persons. What was being felt and how an interaction was being experienced were infinitely more important to him than why such processes might be occurring. Concepts such as the actualizing tendency and self-actualization are merely attempts to offer explanations for the subjective processes which Rogers and his colleagues found themselves repeatedly experiencing when they were able to trust themselves and their clients to meet without preconceived notions about human nature and human development.

In the detailed theoretical exposition of 1959 Rogers emphasizes his belief in the fundamental predominance of the subjective. At one point he even goes so far as to state that although there may exist such a thing as objective truth we can, in fact, never know it. 'There is no such thing as Scientific Knowledge', he says, 'there are only individual perceptions of what appears to each person to be such knowledge' (Rogers, 1959: 192).

Such a cautious approach to the formulation of theory with its deep commitment to the valuing and understanding of subjective experience has many implications. Essentially Rogers was concerned to be as open as possible to his own and his client's experience within the process of the therapeutic relationship. This involved the greatest commitment to understanding the client's inner world from the client's point of view and not from his own. The basic data of therapy could thus be described as the subjective worlds of therapist and client as experienced by each within his or her own framework and the interaction of the two. The theory of psychotherapy and personality change which was eventually constructed arose from the experienced data of the encounter between two subjective worlds in the context of a basically vulnerable or anxious client seeking help from a basically integrated therapist. These experienced data Rogers described as the phenomena of therapy and his theory was an attempt to give order and clarification to the phenomena. The theory seeks to describe what happens and how it happens. The hypotheses which follow from this about the nature of human personality and the dynamics of human behaviour are a further attempt to make sense of the experienced data. They are tentative answers to the 'why' questions. In brief, Rogers' theory about the nature of the therapeutic relationship and the process of personality change within it lead to hypotheses about the nature of human personality and human behaviour. He does not state at the outset that human beings are by definition forward-moving creatures whose total organism manifests an actualizing tendency. Instead he makes the more modest claim that what is discovered by therapist and client in a helping relationship when both give value to subjective experience and perception strongly supports the hypothesis that the human organism shares the same actualizing tendency as is observable in other parts of the natural order. He further hypothesizes that such a tendency is frequently obscured precisely because subjective experience is not valued and cherished in the way that therapeutic relationships can make possible but is instead subjected to criticism and adverse judgements which lead to conditions of worth and a self-actualizing process at odds with the actualizing tendency of the total organism. The crucial issue is that the starting point is experience, by which Rogers came to mean 'all that is going on within the envelope of the organism at any given moment which is potentially available to awareness' (Rogers, 1959: 197).

Rogers on more than one occasion expressed profound regret at what he considered the scurvy treatment that Freud received from his more slavish followers. From his own reading of Freud's work he concluded that Freud was constantly open to new perceptions and experiences and saw his theories as creative but temporary constructs and never more than that. Freud's insecure disciples, however, seized upon the theories and rapidly converted them into dogma of alarming rigidity. For Rogers this not only did Freud a gross disservice, it also underlined the immense danger of any theory that makes it more difficult to be open to new experiences or, indeed, to perceive familiar experiences in new ways. Rogers believed that only one statement could be accurately applied to all theories: that at the time of its formulation every theory enshrines an unknown quantity of error and false inference. Like all truly great men Rogers was essentially humble before the mystery of experience, and in a memorable phrase hoped that he would not suffer the fate of Freud whose 'gossamer threads' of theory had been transformed by his followers into the 'woven chains of dogma' (Rogers, 1959: 191).

3

Rogers' Major Practical Contributions

In his editorial commentary to the special issue of the *Person-Centered Review* celebrating the fiftieth anniversary of client-centred therapy, David Cain commented: 'Rogers' impact . . . on the fields of psychology, psychotherapy, education and human relations in general can be variously described as momentous, persuasive, indirect or elusive' (Cain, 1990: 357). It is true that many of Rogers' theoretical concepts have been absorbed into everyday psychological parlance without any acknowledgement of their origin (for example self-concept, positive regard) and much that was revolutionary in the early years of client-centred therapy is now apparently taken for granted by practitioners of many different therapeutic schools. It is this fact which leads some therapists to believe that person-centred therapy is what everyone does at the outset of a therapeutic relationship before embarking on the *real* therapy which, of course, bears an entirely different brand label.

Such monumental misconceptions angered Rogers considerably for they provided tiresome evidence that there were many who still saw his approach to therapy as consisting merely of certain relationship techniques rather than as a functional philosophy based upon radical convictions about the nature of the human being and of human development. On the other hand, there is a positive side to this widespread and somewhat perverse misunderstanding, for counselling and psychotherapy owe to Carl Rogers the almost universal acceptance of the cardinal importance of the therapeutic relationship as a primary healing agent in therapy. Yet the 'techniques' which are often cited as 'Rogerian' turn out to be nothing less than the art of listening and understanding. Incredible as it may seem, before Rogers and his colleagues embarked on their pioneering work, it was by no means common for therapists to relate closely to their clients let alone for them to listen attentively to what the client had to say and to attempt to understand his or her inner world. Such therapist behaviour was often seen as irrelevant to the diagnosis of mental disturbance and its treatment. Furthermore there were no clients to relate to: they were all *patients* with the inference that, as sick persons, they needed to have things done to them even if what was 'done' was the persuasive use of advice or interpretation through the imposition of words. It was Rogers who first used the word 'client' and thereby conferred on the person in need both respect and a rightful share of power.

Relating, Listening, Understanding

The establishing of the 'core conditions' as necessary and sufficient for therapeutic movement had major practical implications for Rogers and his colleagues. It would be incorrect, however, to relate this to the evolution of *techniques* in client-centred therapy. The word 'technique' suggests an almost mechanical mode of behaviour, something the trainee therapist learns to do as a kind of automatic response to the client. But the core conditions become established not because of what the therapist does but as a result of the attitudes the therapist holds towards his or her client. In short, the therapist is concerned not with the perfecting of techniques but with the expression of attitudes within a given relationship.

Rogers believed that a human being deserves the deepest respect for what he or she *is* no matter how worthless or inadequate he or she may *feel*. He also believed that it was the therapist's task to seek to understand as accurately as possible the client's inner world and to be without façade or guile or the comfort of the protective cloak of professional authority. This clutch of beliefs and attitudes determines the client-centred therapist's way of being with clients, but the actual mode of expression of such beliefs and attitudes will vary considerably from therapist to therapist and will mirror the range of personality differences and variations to be found in any practitioner group. In short, client-centred therapists may differ widely in therapeutic style despite the fact that they all subscribe to the same beliefs about human beings and the desirable characteristics of a therapeutic relationship.

The model of relating which client-centred therapy offers now stands as a challenging reference point for therapists of almost all traditions. Some may wish to imitate it – even if only during the beginning stages of therapy and through the application of responsive 'techniques' – others may wish to embrace certain aspects of it while rejecting others; some, again, may wish to reject it completely as hopelessly idealistic or as promising far more than it can ever in practice deliver. Whatever the response, there can be little doubt that the relationship characterized by the core conditions serves as an inspiration, a challenge, a dangerous heresy or a major irritant for therapists of many different traditions throughout the world.

While it is true that the concept of congruence, with its emphasis on therapist genuineness and the relinquishing of professional power, has received a cool reception in most other therapeutic quarters, the converse is probably true of both empathy and unconditional positive regard in so far as these two attitudes often seem acceptable, at least, in a modified form. Most therapists nowadays like to believe that they are acceptant of their clients and essentially non-judgemental and most pay at least lip-service to the desirability of empathic understanding. Indeed, it is not unusual for therapists schooled in other traditions to discover that responses springing from their acceptance and empathy are powerfully efficacious in bringing about change and for this, in turn, to herald a 'conversion' to a more thoroughgoing person-centred point of view. As a trainer of person-centred therapists I am struck, for example, by the number of would-be trainees who have become disenchanted with other therapeutic traditions and for whom the discovery of the power of acceptance or empathy or both has been the spur to seeking a new professional identity.

Demystifying Therapy

In some ways Rogers' commitment to the relationship as the principal healing agent in therapy is the logical outcome of his belief that being human is a glorious undertaking and that therapists have everything to lose by concealing their humanity behind a mask of psychological knowledge and expertise. From an early stage of his professional career he determined to rescue psychotherapy from those who, for their own reasons, wished to wrap it in mystery and to make it a domain where only those possessing the most prestigious qualifications in medicine, psychiatry or psychology could hope to practise. Rogers believed that therapy was such an important activity that it required opening up to the closest scrutiny and that far from trading on secrecy and mystification it should be revealed in all its observable dimensions. Only in this way, Rogers believed, could therapeutic relationships be subjected to the kind of evaluation which might lead to a fuller understanding of processes and hence to more effective work. Rogers, the person, and Rogers, the scientist, were united in the task of demystifying therapeutic relationships so that they could be studied and experienced as vibrant interactions between real human beings rather than as private, hermetic and essentially mysterious treatment processes between distressed patients and omniscient professionals.

Recording and Filming

One major outcome of this way of thinking was Rogers' pioneering work with the phonographic recording of therapeutic sessions and of whole therapeutic processes. Today, when audio-recording and videotaping have become commonplace, it is difficult to imagine a time when the notion of recording therapeutic interactions verbatim was seen as revolutionary. For many, such procedures constituted a trespassing into the holy of holies and when, later, Rogers allowed himself to be filmed with clients this was an even more threatening innovation for those therapists who preferred to draw a veil of complete secrecy and confidentiality over their therapeutic interactions.

When Rogers began recording interviews in the early 1940s the technical difficulties were formidable. Two phonographs were required so that when one record was being turned over or removed then the other machine could immediately begin recording so that not a single word of the interview was missed. By 1942 Rogers could write that he already had nearly a hundred interviews on record with accompanying typescripts of the therapeutic sessions involved. Then, as now, such recordings proved invaluable in many different ways. They gave a vivid and immediate picture of client attitudes and powerfully illustrated such topics as client resistance and changes in self-perception. They were also effective in highlighting the facilitative responses of therapists and in identifying the inhibiting behaviours which tended to halt or impede the therapeutic process. Their value in the training of therapists proved inestimable and the process of supervision was enhanced beyond measure. It is no exaggeration to suggest that Rogers' introduction of recording technology into the counselling room not only engendered whole new areas for research and training methodology but also paved the way for the opening up of therapeutic processes to public scrutiny to the immense benefit of many clients and would-be clients. The not infrequent opportunities which millions of people have nowadays to observe therapy sessions on the television screen are a direct outcome of Rogers' innovative procedures of fifty years ago.

A further benefit of recordings is the preservation for posterity of many examples of Carl Rogers himself working with clients. The significance of this cannot be overemphasized, for there must be literally thousands of therapists working today, not only in the person-centred tradition, who have had the experience of listening to Rogers in dialogue with individual clients or of seeing him on the cinema or video screen. Rogers was courageous enough to put himself 'on the line' in this way and the result of such courage and the power of the influence he exerted as a result are incalculable.

Most significantly, the existence of recordings and films means that the concepts of congruence, unconditional positive regard and empathy do not remain theoretical constructs, admirable only for their intellectual elegance and succinctness. On repeated occasions Rogers embodied the concepts on the tapes and films, which provide countless examples of what it means to be living out the person-centred approach as a functional philosophy. The experience of listening to or watching Carl Rogers being empathic, congruent and unconditionally accepting is unforgettable and it could be argued that the tapes and films he made which have been distributed to all corners of the globe have constituted one of the major contributions to the understanding and development of counselling psychology in the last twenty years.

Rogers and His Famous Clients

Herbert Bryan

It has been suggested (Kirschenbaum and Henderson, 1990a: 61) that no single volume did more to influence the practice of counselling and psychotherapy in the United States than Rogers' *Counseling and Psychotherapy*, published in 1942. Be this as it may, the outstanding feature of the book was the inclusion of the first recorded, fully transcribed and published psychotherapy case in history. Herbert Bryan is the first of Rogers' clients to be made famous throughout the world by their appearance in his books, on audio-recordings or on film. Unlike clients drawn from the case books of other well-known therapists, Herbert Bryan is not presented through the eyes of his therapist. He appears in his own words so that the reader can engage with him directly: Rogers, too, appears not through the filter of recollection but through the words and responses of the moment-to-moment relationship with his client. Nothing is hidden and Rogers in his commentary on their dialogue is utterly non-defensive about his own performance. He openly speaks of blunders, and two such instances taken from the first session with Herbert Bryan are particularly revealing. In both cases, Rogers chastises himself for interrupting his client's flow or recognition of feeling, something he does on each occasion by posing direct questions. He comments on his first intervention, which actually interrupted Mr Bryan when he was in full flow:

'Why did the counselor interrupt here? This seems to be a quite unnecessary directive question breaking into the flow of feeling.'

The second occasion shows Rogers as even more self-critical. Mr Bryan is exploring issues of motivation and energy and is wishing that his negative forces were not so much in the ascendancy. He is wondering how he can possibly change the 'balance of power' within himself. He says:

> Well, to draw another analogy, I feel that I have so much energy, so much reservoir of energy – now, what I want to do is to get the negatives to desert to the positive side. Which will be a double-barrelled gain, you see, and will probably occur very rapidly once the ball gets rolling. But when the negatives are in power, why, of course, how can the ball begin to roll?

Rogers' response follows immediately: 'Can you, uh – not today, but one question that you may want to be thinking over is, what are these negative roles?'

In his commentary Rogers refers to his response as 'the second blunder of the hour'. The reason for this critical judgement is the same as before: 'the counselor departs from sound recognition of feeling'. Instead of some such response as 'You feel that someone else must start the ball rolling', he asks a direct question which goes deep into the client's situation. If Mr Bryan were fully aware of why his 'negative' side was in power, he would have little need of help. The counselor draws nothing but a 'confused and somewhat defensive answer'.

Rogers' concern to underline the inappropriateness of these two responses springs from the central importance he placed on accompanying rather than leading the client and on the empathic responsiveness which is required if the client is to be enabled to stay in touch with and to explore his or her feelings. Time and again in his recorded interviews Rogers demonstrates what is involved if the client's inner world is to be deeply understood by the therapist. Recognizing feelings and allowing them free expression is crucial to the empathic enterprise and certain therapist responses facilitate such a process whereas others impede it. Directive questions are seldom helpful whereas other modes of response encourage the process and enable the client to be more in touch with his experiencing. In another part of the interview, Mr Bryan is trying to describe a complex and elusive sensation.

> *H.B.* Well, I don't know if I can any more accurately describe the sensation. It's just a – a very impressive and painful weight as if an axe were pressing on the whole abdomen, pressing down, I can almost – I can almost sense the position and I feel that's

oppressing me very radically, that is, that it goes right down to the roots of my dynamic energy, so that no matter in what field I essay any sort of effort, I find the blocking.

C.R.   It really just cripples you as far as anything else is concerned.

H.B.   Yes, Mmmhm. And that even has a physical counterpart. When I walk, that is, when I'm feeling badly, I walk hunched over and sort of like I had a bellyache, which I actually do have, psychologically.

C.R.   Mmhm. It just makes you more or less half a man, is that it? And only half able to do your work –

H.B.   Yes. It's just as if I had an axe in me literally, you might say. I feel it in my very core of energy – it's blocked and oppressed in that painful way. It's a deep-seated thing, because conversely when I get the release I feel a deep-seated flowing of energy.

C.R.   When you feel all right – you feel very much all right.

H.B.   Oh, yes, yes. Very dynamic – my mind works much more rapidly and everything's all right. Anything I try, I do successfully.

C.R.   And what you want is to find ways of increasing the amount of time that you have that dynamic self, is that it?

H.B.   Oh, yes. Be that way all the time. I don't see any reason why I couldn't be. The whole thing is psychological and I want to get at it. (Rogers, 1942: 265–87)

In this sequence Rogers, with apparently effortless ease, is doing precisely what he criticizes himself for *not* doing on the other two occasions. He is recognizing feeling in Mr Bryan and allowing the feeling to be deepened and differentiated. He shows himself as the sensitive companion and not as the somewhat authoritative interrogator. In such a climate Mr Bryan is released into showing something of the 'dynamic self' which he would like to be all the time. This brief example of empathic responsiveness can be replicated on innumerable occasions from recorded interviews that Rogers made and there was a period when empathy came almost to be defined as the capacity to reflect feelings. Indeed, in a letter to Rogers, John Shlien of Harvard could write in 1986: 'It [reflection of feeling] is an instrument of artistic virtuosity in the hands of a sincere, intelligent, empathic listener. It made possible the development of client-centred therapy, when the philosophy alone could not have.'

Significantly, Rogers himself was much less happy with the term 'reflection of feeling' and it was his very unhappiness which prompted Shlien to offer his spirited defence of the concept. Rogers remained unconvinced, but Shlien's enthusiasm brought him to what he termed a 'double insight'. In the *Person-Centered Review* of November 1986 he wrote:

From my point of view as a therapist, I am *not* trying to 'reflect feelings'. I am trying to determine whether my understanding of the client's inner world is correct – whether I am seeing it as he or she is experiencing it at this moment. Each response of mine contains the unspoken question, 'Is this the way it is in you? Am I catching just the colour and texture and flavor of the personal meaning you are experiencing right now? If not, I wish to bring my perception in line with yours.' On the other hand, I know from the client's point of view we are holding up a mirror to his or her current experiencing. The feelings and personal meanings seem sharper when seen through the eyes of another, when they are reflected.

So I suggest that these therapist responses be labeled not 'Reflections of Feeling', but 'Testing Understandings', or 'Checking Perceptions'. Such terms would, I believe, be more accurate. They would be helpful in the training of therapists. They would supply a sound motivation in responding, a questioning desire rather than an intent to 'reflect'. (Rogers, 1986d: 375–7)

Whether we term therapist responses of this kind 'Reflections of Feeling' or 'Testing Understandings' is immaterial. Their significance lies in the fact that they typify what it meant for Rogers to translate the notion of empathy into therapeutic practice. They demonstrate the sensitive artistry of a therapist who realized that the inner world of another cannot be grasped without, on the therapist's part, both the questioning desire and the capacity to facilitate the flow and expression of feeling. In the relationship with Herbert Bryan, as in so many others recorded later, Rogers shows what is involved in entering the perceptual world of another person and acknowledges that the task can easily be undermined by the therapist's impatience or inability to resist the urge to lead or direct.

It is interesting that in the discussion quoted above Rogers draws attention to the usefulness of a term such as 'Testing Understandings' as far as the training of therapists is concerned. Rogers was in many ways an incurable educator; he hoped to influence therapeutic practice through his recordings and films and realized that such material could serve an important function in training programmes. His disillusionment with much therapist training was well known and he was particularly horrified by the often total lack of emphasis on the development of a trainee's empathic abilities. It is difficult to imagine, however, that anyone could hear Rogers in action or read a transcript of a therapy session in which he was involved without becoming deeply aware of the powerful efficacy of empathic responsiveness. Rogers also showed that empathy demands of the therapist a willingness to marshal the full range of emotional and cognitive abilities both to understand the client and to convey that understanding. Rogers' recordings provide compelling evidence of empathy in operation and, as such, their influence on the therapeutic practice of others is incalculable.

Gloria

In 1964 Rogers was filmed in a half-hour interview with Gloria, an attractive 30 year old divorcee. It was an astonishing encounter, for in this brief space of time, Rogers succeeded in exemplifying almost all the key elements of client-centred therapy. The power of the interview is reflected by the fact that Gloria continued to maintain intermittent contact with Rogers until her death many years later. She rates as one of the most renowned clients in the history of psychotherapy and her contribution to the understanding and practice of client-centred therapy throughout the world is considerable. Her state of readiness for therapy was such that Rogers was able in the space of a mere half-hour not only to establish the climate for growth characterized by the presence of the core conditions but also to accompany Gloria to the point where she experienced her own feelings in the moment and entered deeply into a person-to-person relationship. The Gloria film contributes a major and incontrovertible piece of evidence for the effectiveness of client-centred therapy; it is also an astonishing demonstration of what in practical and experiential terms it means to be acceptant, empathic and congruent in a therapeutic relationship.

There is, of course, no substitute for the actual experience of watching the film of Rogers at work with Gloria. In almost all ways film is an ideal medium for conveying the elusive nature of the implementation of attitudes. Clearly, too, Rogers demonstrates what it means for *him* to be acceptant, empathic and congruent and the film provides, in this respect, a record of one man's particular style of being in a therapeutic relationship. Nonetheless, there is a universal validity about the interaction for it presents with memorable poignancy what it means to participate in the creation of a 'climate for growth'. In addition, Gloria's concerns are such that she serves as a powerful example of the anguish that arises when the essential actualizing tendency of the organism finds itself in conflict with the need to actualize the self and to preserve a self-concept worthy of respect and approval.

The depth of this anguish is revealed in the opening minutes of the interview, when Gloria tells Rogers of her acute difficulties in adjusting to a single life. Her natural striving to meet her needs through sexual expression is in direct conflict with her concept of herself as a person with 'proper' sexual behaviour who never lies. The conflict reaches its climax as she finds herself lying to her 9-year-old daughter about her sexual behaviour because she does not wish the child to be adversely affected by her permissive life-style.

The guilt feelings in Gloria are uppermost at the outset, and throughout the interview she struggles to come to terms with the person she is and to achieve the kind of self-acceptance which will enable her to be honest with herself and with her daughter. At first she externalizes the problem by focusing on the potential effect of her behaviour on her daughter and asking Rogers for his guidance. As the interview proceeds, however, she finds the courage to face her own incongruence (the bifurcation of the actualizing tendency), to live her feelings in the moment and to recognize that her basis for evaluation must be inside herself. The process moves with astonishing rapidity and is characterized by a deepening intensity of feeling and by an openness to each other of therapist and client which often moves audiences watching the film to the verge of tears.

Throughout the interview Rogers repeatedly shows the empathic responsiveness which informs all his therapeutic work, but in some ways the film conveys with even greater effectiveness the quality of his acceptance and the utter genuineness of his presence. For Gloria, who is tormented by guilt feelings and who vainly seeks an authority outside herself, Rogers' acceptance and complete lack of 'professional' façade are critically important. His warm and sensitive accompanying of her feelings, the total absence of negative judgement and his willingness to reveal himself as a person enable her to find the courage to explore her inner world ever more deeply and to discover her own 'locus of evaluation'. Two extracts from the interview serve to illuminate the intensity of Rogers' 'companionship' of the client with particular force. The first is taken from the opening minutes of the interview, the second from near the end.

With the focus very much on the relationship with her daughter, Pammy, Gloria is struggling with how her daughter would react if she really knew the truth about her mother's sexual behaviour. Rogers gently sums up her dilemma:

Rogers: . . . If she really knew you, would she, could she accept you?
Gloria: This is what I don't know, I don't want her to turn away from me. I don't even know how I feel about it because there are times when I feel so guilty like when I have a man over, I even try to make a special set-up so that if I were ever alone with him, the children would never catch me in that sort of thing. Because I'm real leery about it. And yet I also know that I have these desires.
Rogers: And so it is quite clear that it isn't only her problem or the relationship with her, it's in you as well.
Gloria: In my guilt. I feel guilty so often.
Rogers: 'What can I accept myself as doing?' And you realize that with these sort of subterfuges, so as to make sure that you're not

caught or something, you realize that you are acting from guilt, is that it?

Gloria: Yes, and I don't like the . . . I would like to feel comfortable with whatever I do. If I choose not to tell Pammy the truth, to feel comfortable that she can handle it, and I don't. I want to be honest, and yet I feel there are some areas that *I* don't even accept.

Rogers: And if you can't accept them in yourself, how could you possibly be comfortable in telling them to her?

Gloria: Right.

Rogers: And yet, as you say, you do have these desires and you do have your feelings, but you don't feel good about them.

Gloria: Right. I have a feeling that you are just going to sit there and let me stew in it and I want more. I want you to help me get rid of my guilt feelings. If I can get rid of my guilt feelings about lying or going to bed with a single man, any of that, just so I can feel more comfortable.

Rogers: And I guess I'd like to say, 'No, I don't want to let you stew in your feelings', but on the other hand, I also feel that this is the kind of very private thing that I couldn't possibly answer *for* you. But I sure as anything will try to help you work toward your own answer. I don't know whether that makes any sense to you, but I mean it. (Shostrom, 1965)

In this passage Rogers enables Gloria to face the conflict in herself and shares in her pain. He does not ignore her direct request for help but, as he expresses concern and understanding of her dilemma, he affirms his belief in her ability to discover her own way forward and promises to help her find the answers within herself. His deep desire to be with her radiates from his whole being and there is no recourse to professional language or to clever analysis. 'I sure as anything will try to help you work toward your own answer' is a passionate statement of intent from a man who believes equally passionately in his client's capacity to find her own way through life.

Towards the end of the interview Gloria is speaking of 'utopian' moments when she feels 'right' about herself and is able to trust the feelings that rise up in her as accurate guides to behaviour. Rogers is clearly moved by her recognition of organismic harmony:

Rogers: I sense that in those utopian moments you really feel kind of whole. You feel all in one piece. . .

Gloria: Yes, it gives me a choked up feeling when you say that because I don't get that as often as I'd like. I like that whole feeling. That's real precious to me.

Rogers: I expect none of us get it as often as we'd like, but I really do understand it. [*pause. Tears come to her eyes.*] That really does touch you doesn't it?

Gloria: Yes, and you know what else I was just thinking? I – a dumb thing – that all of a sudden while I was talking to you I thought, 'Gee, how nice I can talk to you and I want you to approve of me and I respect you, but I miss that my father couldn't talk to me like you are.' I mean, I'd like to say, 'Gee, I'd like you for my father'. I don't even know why that came to me.

Rogers: You look to me like a pretty nice daughter. But you really do miss the fact that you couldn't be open with your own dad. (Shostrom, 1965)

This passage has achieved a certain notoriety and much nonsense has been talked about Rogers' inability to 'work with the transference'. The very mention of such a concept shows a failure to recognize entirely what has happened in the relationship. So deep is the trust that Gloria has developed in her therapist that she is able to move into an intensity of feeling which reveals Rogers to her as the father she never had. Rogers, for his part, does not attempt to evade or reject the intensity. On the contrary, he reciprocates by attending closely to the feelings inside himself: 'You look to me like a pretty nice daughter.' This response further cements the relationship and in the closing minutes of the interview Gloria is able to reflect upon her feelings for her father and upon her deep sadness at his inability to offer her the love and understanding she craves. Gently, Rogers acknowledges the depth of her hurt:

Rogers: You feel that 'I am permanently cheated'.
Gloria: That is why I like substitutes. Like I like talking to you and I like men that I can respect. Doctors, and I keep sort of underneath a feeling like we are real close, you know, sort of like a substitute father.
Rogers: I don't feel that's pretending.
Gloria: Well, you are not really my father.
Rogers: No, I meant about the real close business.
Gloria: Well, see, I sort of feel that's pretending, too, because I can't expect you to feel very close to me. You don't know me that well.
Rogers: All I know is what I'm feeling, and that is I feel close to you in this moment. (Shostrom, 1965).

This closing passage shows Rogers at his most transparent and illustrates his refusal to be anything other than himself in the moment. Clearly he could have acknowledged the obvious truth of Gloria's comment that he is not her father and that they are both acquaintances of half an hour. Instead, despite the fact that the interview is at an end, he affirms the closeness and the affection which he feels for Gloria. He offers her the truth of his own experiencing and in that moment he eschews all 'professionalism' in the interests of the authenticity which is, for him, the cornerstone of the person-centred therapist's new professionalism founded not on psychological expertise but on the capacity to be fully human.

Jan

More than twenty years after the film with Gloria, Rogers gave a demonstration therapy session to a workshop of 600 participants in Johannesburg, South Africa. Several people had volunteered and it was left to Rogers' colleague, Ruth Sanford, to select a client. Jan was chosen and the session was recorded. Subsequently Rogers himself decided to reflect on the interview and to write about it (Rogers, 1986b). In many ways Gloria and Jan might well have been clients seen on the same day in 1964, for little seems to have changed in Rogers' operational functioning as a therapist. Indeed in a recent article Jerold Bozarth has argued that throughout his career Rogers neither altered his fundamental view of therapy nor changed his way of being in a therapeutic relationship (Bozarth, 1990: 61). Through careful analysis of various demonstration recordings made over the years Bozarth concludes that Rogers' interviews with clients were predominantly dedicated to the unspoken question, 'Is this the way it is in you?' In other words, his therapeutic relationships were characterized primarily by what we have called 'empathic responsiveness'.

In one important respect, however, the interview with Jan differs significantly from its predecessors and it is tempting to believe that Rogers' decision to write about it may well have been prompted by this new element. Some way into the interview Jan comments on the amateur dramatics in which she used to be involved:

> Jan: This may be related, and it may be able to help you: whether it's something to do with the amateur dramatics that I used to be involved with, I don't know, but I love playing the naughty little girl. And whenever I want to get away with something or I want something, I would play that naughty little girl.
>
> Rogers: That's a part that you know very well. [*Jan laughs.*] You've acted it in many plays. [*Jan: And it works*] It *works* – the naughty little girl can get away with things . . .

A few minutes later Jan begins to experience a great sense of hopelessness and expresses her yearning for a helping relationship with another person and her conviction that help must come from outside.

> Rogers: . . .you wish so much that there was this other person from outside, who would give you confidence, who could help you through this tough time.
>
> Jan: Yes, because although I do pray – I have my own feelings about religion – I believe in spiritual development. And maybe

for me this is a karmic conditioning, I don't know. That's another thing, of course, that's going on in my mind: it's a part of my development, as it were. But I feel it's not enough; I must have physical contact. [*Pause*]. Somebody I can relate to . . .

Rogers: Somebody you can relate to. And I guess that – this may seem like a silly idea, but – I wish that one of those friends could be that naughty little girl. I don't know whether that makes any sense to you or not, but if that kind of sprightly, naughty little girl that lives inside could accompany you from the light into the dark – as I say, that may not make any sense to you at all.

Jan: [*In a puzzled voice.*] Can you elaborate on that a little more for me?

Rogers: Simply that maybe one of your best friends is the you that you hide inside, the fearful little girl, the naughty little girl, the real you that doesn't come out very much in the open.

Jan: [*Pause*] And I must admit – what you have just said, and looking at it in retrospect – I've lost a lot of that naughty little girl. In fact, over the last eighteen months, that naughty little girl has disappeared.

Rogers, in his commentary on this passage, is highly excited because for the first time he has captured on a recording what he calls an 'intuitive' response. Such responses, he believes, arise out of a slightly altered state of consciousness when he is 'indwelling in the client's world, completely in tune with that world'. His introduction of the 'naughty little girl' is not a conscious affair but is a response that arises in him from his 'nonconscious sensing of the world of the other'.

It is evident that the intuitive response which Rogers values so highly is the outcome of the quality of 'presence' of which he wrote briefly towards the end of his life and to which he attributed 'transcendental' and 'spiritual' dimensions. It is also significant that he finds himself offering the intuitive, nonconscious response immediately following Jan's own reference to her practice of prayer and her belief in spiritual development. The suspicion that it was this one passage which persuaded Rogers to offer his work with Jan to posterity is further strengthened by his concluding comment in his reflections on the interview.

The next morning Jan told me that the interchange about the 'naughty little girl' had initiated a self-searching. She realized that not only was the naughty little girl missing, but several other parts of her self had also disappeared during the past eighteen months. 'I realize that to face life as a whole person I need to find those missing parts of me.' She said that for her the interview had proved to be a 'soul-shaking experience'. (Rogers, 1986b: 197–208)

The language of spiritual development, intuitive responses and soul-shaking signifies new terrain both for Carl Rogers and for his clients and yet this brief excursion into the world of 'indwelling' where intuition can be trusted may yet prove to be a major practical contribution from the man whose favourite saint was Thomas, the Doubter (Thorne, 1990: 396).

⌐ The Precursor of Client-centred Practice

The practice of client-centred therapy constituted a radical departure from most of what passed for therapy at the time of its original evolution. It blazed a new trail that differed markedly from both the psychoanalytical and behavioural traditions. Rogers' profound respect for the client's capacity to find his or her own answers, once the necessary psychological conditions were established, led to an apparent simplicity of practice which often masked, to the uninitiated, the enormous demands placed upon the therapist. Rogers saw no need to probe deeply into the client's unconscious and he believed there were great dangers in offering interpretations, however insightful, or in attempting, for example, to analyse dreams. Furthermore he abhorred behavioural manipulations and was sceptical about the use of psychological tests if the aim was to diagnose or label problems. His concern was to establish an honest relationship with his clients, characterized by an unpossessive caring and a deep empathic responsiveness. Although the essential ideas of the person-centred approach are without complexity, implementation of these ideas can be challenging in the extreme.

We have already noted the influence of Otto Rank on the child guidance colleagues who were close to Rogers during his formative years at Rochester. Jessie Taft and Frederick Allen were renowned for their profound respect for Rank's ideas and Taft was to write a book on Rank in the late 1950s (Taft, 1958). It seems likely that it was not only Rank's theoretical ideas which were powerful and influential among child guidance practitioners at this time but also his actual practice of therapy. In James Liebermann's expressive account of Rank's life and work (Liebermann, 1985) there are several allusions to Rank's behaviour with his patients and he, like Rogers after him, believed deeply in the worthiness of the person and in the patient's capacity for finding his or her own way forward. He wrote that he applied 'no general therapy or theory. I let the patient work on his own psychology, as it were' (Rank, 1966: 17). Liebermann quotes a student of Rank as saying in 1938, 'the actual therapeutic relationship is the curative factor', and a patient who reported that 'nothing was imposed on you. Rank was not looking for a disease, he was not trying to eradicate anything. He wanted you to open up and be as you might want to be but didn't dare to' (Liebermann, 1985: xxxvi). It is not difficult to surmise from these brief remarks that Otto Rank, too, saw his approach as a functional philosophy and that, in practice, he showed the same open and accessible response to those seeking his help as client-centred therapists of later years. If Rogers gave shape and form to an idea whose time had come, as he himself was to put it, Otto Rank may justifiably be seen as the theoretician who paved the way for much that became central to person-centred theory and as a clinician whose practice was to be reflected and developed in the later work of Rogers and his colleagues.

The Lay Therapist

In 1973 Rogers was awarded the Distinguished Professional Contribution Award by the American Psychological Association and he gave an address to mark the occasion at the Association's annual meeting. He chose to look back over forty-six years of professional activity and to identify his most significant struggles and achievements. Despite the honour which had been bestowed upon him by his fellow psychologists Rogers was quick to note that academic psychology found him painfully embarrassing.

> The science and profession of psychology have, I believe, profoundly ambivalent feelings about me and my work. I am seen – and here I must rely mostly on hearsay – as softheaded, unscientific, cultish, too easy on students, full of strange and upsetting enthusiasms about ephemeral things like the self, therapist attitudes, and encounter groups. I have defamed the most holy mysteries of the academic – the professional lecture and the whole evaluation system – from the ABCs of course grades to the coveted hood of the doctor's degree. (Rogers, 1974a: 116)

Later in the same address Rogers describes, with obvious relish, his ferocious battles with members of the psychiatric profession, many of whom had attempted to prevent mere psychologists from practising psychotherapy at all. He tells of one aggressively hostile psychiatrist at the University of Chicago who had demanded that the Counseling Center be closed since its members were practising medicine (that is, psychotherapy) without a licence. Rogers' response to such opposition from the medical profession was either to mount a blistering counterattack or to move ahead with such speed in theory, research and practice that the pre-eminence of psychologists in the therapeutic arena was indisputable. About such matters he was implacable, and he confessed that his behaviour in what he often believed to be an all-out war was deeply surprising and even shocking to those who were more accustomed to see his thoughtful and gentle side.

It is not difficult to understand why Rogers so frequently provoked the anger of professional power groups, whether academic, medical or political. He had no confidence that academic qualifications, medical expertise or even psychological sophistication endowed people with the capacity to help others. There was even evidence to suggest that the weighty baggage of intellectual and academic achievement could diminish rather than augment an individual's ability to relate to others. By his emphasis on the personal qualities of therapists Rogers threatened those whose professional identity depended on the length of their training or their accumulation of higher degrees. On the other hand, his point of view was immensely encouraging and supportive to those who might otherwise have considered it impossible to pursue careers as therapists.

Rogers' impassioned insistence on the primary importance of the therapist's personal qualities opened up psychotherapy to the psychology profession and contributed to the development of lay therapy in general. The word 'counselling' was originally used by Rogers as another cheeky strategy to silence psychiatrists who were objecting to psychologists practising psychotherapy. By simply changing the name of the activity he enabled practitioners to continue their work without any change in their situation and without detriment to their clients. In our own country the healthy outcome of Rogers' determined campaign has been the evolution of a counselling profession where practitioners are drawn from a wide variety of disciplines and where neither medicine nor psychology rule the roost. Furthermore, the basic attitudes of the client-centred therapist underpin the work of countless individuals who exercise counselling skills in a variety of settings throughout education, the health professions, social work, industry and commerce, the armed services and international organizations. Rogers' indirect contribution to the daily life of literally thousands of individuals who have never heard his name is, by any criterion, astonishing.

Rogers the Researcher

Rogers' research activities during the 1940s, 1950s and 1960s were prolific and the client-centred hypotheses were strengthened and elaborated by the completion and publication of numerous studies undertaken under his general guidance and inspiration. This body of research constituted the most intensive investigation of psychotherapy attempted anywhere in the world up to that time and showed that the delicate and elusive movement of therapeutic processes could be studied and measured purposefully. The major achievement of these studies was to establish beyond all question that psychotherapy could and should be subjected to the rigours of scientific enquiry.

Once he left the university world Rogers' interest in and opportunities for research diminished, but towards the end of his life he returned to the subject with a renewed urgency. In the earlier period he was instrumental in evolving research designs which enabled the objective measurement of the self-concept, ideal self and the relationship of the two over the course of therapy or the correlation of subjective and externally based variables. He also used refined methodologies to explore therapist effectiveness which often involved the introduction of outside consultants and the development of rating scales. These were major innovations which profoundly affected psychology research for many years. In 1961 he wrote in *On Becoming a Person*:

> Therapy is the experience in which I can let myself go subjectively. Research is the experience in which I can stand off and try to view this rich subjective experience with objectivity, applying all the elegant methods of science to determine whether I have been deceiving myself. The conviction grows in me that we shall discover laws of personality and behaviour which are as significant for human progress or human understanding as the law of gravity or the laws of thermodynamics. (Rogers, 1961: 14)

These are the words of a man whose confidence in the objective scientific method is still unshaken and who remains convinced that a rich harvest of discovery lies ahead. The later Rogers, however, speaks with a markedly different voice. Whereas in the 1950s and 1960s he made perhaps *the* major contribution to the objective investigation of therapeutic processes and thereby inspired countless research studies, his contribution in the 1980s is of an entirely different order. In an article published in the *Journal of Humanistic Psychology* in 1985 he finally turns his back on the logical positivism in which he has been professionally reared and unequivocably makes the case for a 'New Science' (Rogers, 1985).

In this article Rogers throws his weight behind forms of investigation which are no longer constrained by the 'straitjacket of logical empiricism'. He cites numerous studies which experiment with new methodologies and new paradigms for doing research. He commends the British book *Human Inquiry: A Sourcebook of New Paradigm Research* by Peter Reason and John Rowan (1981) and refers to it as 'an excellent collection of papers exploring the philosophical and methodological aspects of the new alternative scientific models. It is a gold mine. . .'. With obvious delight he emphasizes a characteristic that seems to link all the new methodologies of which he so firmly approves and in doing so he acknowledges the profound influence of the British scientist, Michael Polanyi, for whom he had great respect and affection. The new methodologies, he suggests, are all infused by Polanyi's term, 'indwelling'. The scientist whom Rogers now commends and encourages develops a 'mode of indwelling' in the world of the participant or participants who are no longer 'subjects' of research but 'research partners' or 'co-researchers'. It is the knowledge gained from this deep empathic indwelling that the researcher will then hope to organize in a purposeful fashion so that new discoveries can be made and new approaches to the truth illuminated (Rogers, 1985: 7–14).

It is not fanciful, I believe, to see in Rogers' clear and enthusiastic endorsement of new research paradigms the inevitable conclusion to a life dedicated to the understanding and validating of subjective experience. No longer is he content to pay even lip-service to the supremacy of the conventional view of science, the Newtonian, mechanistic, linear cause–effect understanding of reality. He does not throw it out but considers it singularly inappropriate for exploring the questions that now need to be addressed in the psychotherapeutic relationship where living human persons deserve to have researchers who are prepared to commit themselves to their studies in a way that enhances the dignity of everyone involved. Throughout his long professional life Rogers devoted himself tirelessly to the pursuit of truth and his research endeavours were highly practical contributions to that quest. As an old man without a research base in an academic institution, his zeal remained unimpaired and his powerful endorsement of new scientific paradigms inspired by empathic indwelling may yet prove to be a powerfully practical contribution to the future of psychotherapeutic research.

Conclusion

It was my privilege to know Carl Rogers and to work with him on a number of occasions in different parts of the world. He always gave of himself unstintingly but never to the detriment of his own being. He was immediately approachable and accessible and yet he knew how to guard and preserve his own privacy. He was a shrewd and penetrating thinker but there was nothing about him of the ivory-tower professor: on the contrary, he was always acutely aware of practical issues and the importance of detailed planning. He was one of life's eternal learners, concerned to develop his own understanding and to facilitate the learning of others. It was for this reason that he wrote so many books and articles, because in doing so he learned more of what he really thought and believed and simultaneously made those thoughts and beliefs available to others. His demonstration therapy sessions served the same function for he loved to set out on the unknown venture of meeting another human being and to do so in a context where not only he and the client but also many others could draw value from the experience. In a way his whole life was a 'contribution', freely and consciously offered to the human family for which he continued to have such hope despite its follies and apparent destructiveness. Above all, perhaps, he was a supremely practical man who was consistently concerned with what 'worked' and who never ceased to ask his clients and his colleagues if he was understanding them aright. For this reason he has left behind a body of knowledge and a way of being which are deeply influential because they are solidly grounded in experience and are the outcome of a life lived to the full.

For Rogers, the human psyche remained a complex mystery to which empathic listening provided one of the least clouded windows. But he did not allow himself to be seduced into developing abstract and untestable theories. Instead he was content to make only low-level inferences and to formulate testable hypotheses. At heart he remained in many ways the agriculturist of his youth and we have every reason to be grateful that a man so dedicated to the exploration of subjective reality could at the same time have his feet so firmly planted on the ground.

4

Criticisms and Rebuttals

Criticisms

Rogers had his critics from the very beginning and they have not grown less vociferous with the passage of the years. At the present time the standing of person-centred scholars and therapists within the world of academic psychology is not high: they tend to be patronized as naive enthusiasts from a former age or to suffer the greatest indignity of all – indifference. Certainly the person-centred viewpoint does not align itself easily with the spirit of the age. We live at a time when the pressure of life encourages swift answers to problems, the application of slick techniques and, above all, procedures which are demonstrably cost effective. In such a climate experts are sought after who can provide authoritative guidance and effect rapid change. Rogers, with his insistence on the uniqueness of individuals and with his unshakeable faith in the capacity of persons to find their own answers, is not a natural hero for the age. His profound distrust of the power-hungry ambitions of many in the helping professions makes him the natural enemy of those who would ply their therapeutic wares in the competitive market-place in order to convince prospective clients that the wonder cure has arrived and that they possess it.

If Rogers' standing in academia is currently at a low ebb, his influence on therapists throughout the world seems to be curiously persistent. Practitioners from many different therapeutic traditions acknowledge their indebtedness and in 1982 a survey of American therapists revealed him as, for them, the most influential figure in twentieth-century psychotherapy, surpassing even Freud (Kirschenbaum and Henderson, 1990a: xiii). In some sense it seems that he has become an idealized figure symbolizing a 'purity' of approach and a hopefulness about both people and therapy which somehow continues to inspire other practitioners even if they openly disagree with his theories and denigrate client-centred practice as altogether too utopian or too demanding in its claims on the therapist's commitment. It is a strange and confusing picture which has its origins in the criticisms thrown at the early pioneers, who were accused at one and the same time of 'doing nothing' in their 'non-directive' therapy and of encouraging a narcissistic ego inflation in their clients. Rogers was castigated throughout his career for being both ineffective and too effective.

Power Issues

⋇ Rogers' ideas threaten those whose professional identity resides chiefly in their psychological knowledge and in their capacity to embody the role of 'expert'. He consistently maintained that the therapist's competence derives not from his or her level of knowledge but from the ability to offer a particular kind of relationship in which the client can gradually move to a new self-concept and way of being. Rogers' persistent battles with the medical and psychiatric professions and the ambivalence he experienced from his fellow psychologists are powerful evidence of the fear he instilled in those who sensed that his theories and practice might undermine their authority and credibility. It is small wonder that they sought to discredit him and even to suggest that he was behaving irresponsibly in encouraging his clients to determine their own way forward. Profound issues of power are at stake in these conflicts and the accusations of superficiality or of irresponsibility are a scarcely veiled attempt to silence someone who calls into question the authority of psychological knowledge and the right of any therapist to diagnose mental conditions – let alone to prescribe courses of treatment. The radical belief that it is the client who knows what hurts and how to find healing throws a mighty spanner in the works for those who see it as their task to evaluate 'conditions' and to set up programmes to remedy problems and to alleviate pain. The tendency of those who feel threatened in this way is to accuse Rogers of misguided naivety and to ridicule him for daring to suppose (for example) that therapeutic relationships can be offered by those with no formal psychological education.

It would be utterly wrong, of course, to maintain that Rogers in reality saw the therapist as a non-expert. On the contrary, he believed that the highest level of expertise was required by anyone who was bold enough to offer psychological assistance to another human being. It was the precise nature of this expertise, however, which concerned him deeply; he saw it as residing not in the therapist's cognitive or even experiential knowledge but in his or her capacity to offer clients a relationship where growth could take place. He believed that such a capacity demanded dedicated commitment on the part of the therapist together with a willingness to develop a rigorous discipline of self-exploration which would ensure a high level of congruence, empathy and acceptance. To those critics who accuse Rogers of selling psychotherapy short and reducing it to the level of a mere loving relationship it should be pointed out that such a relationship, marked as it is by the involvement of the therapist's total responsiveness, is rare in the extreme and constitutes not a cheapening but an elevation of psychotherapy to an altogether different plane of experience.

Human Nature: Criticisms of Rogers' Viewpoint
Rogers' trust in the client is buttressed by and indeed dependent upon his beliefs about the essential nature of the human being and these beliefs have often come in for the severest criticism from the same people who feel their own power base threatened by the person-centred philosophy. Depending on your viewpoint, it is clearly naive to trust persons if you believe that they are by definition untrustworthy or behaviourally conditioned or corrupt or a mass of potentially destructive instinctual drives. Such beliefs and others equally denigratory of human personality are held by many of Rogers' critics in both the psychological and theological domains.

Rogers, as we have seen, makes clear assumptions about human nature and emphasizes that humans are growth oriented and will naturally progress towards the fulfilment of their innate potential if psychological conditions are favourable. By contrast, Freud in *Civilization and Its Discontents* (1930) portrays men and women as essentially 'savage beasts' whose aggressive tendencies and unpredictable sexuality can only be domesticated by the processes and structures of civilization. Freud was pessimistic about human nature and saw the instinctual drives as pushing individuals towards the selfish satisfaction of primitive needs or the relief of powerful tensions. This gloomy view is supported and reinforced by the strong emphasis which Freud placed on the unconscious with its powerfully destructive elements. The primary significance of the unconscious sources of human disturbance and unhappiness characterizes the analytical point of view in its many varieties – neo-Freudian and otherwise – and even when the unconscious is seen as the repository of many positive forces (as, for instance, in the work of Carl Jung) there often remains the predominant sense of a human nature which is essentially unpredictable, untrustworthy and in continual need of careful monitoring and control. Not surprisingly, therefore, many analytical theorists regard Rogers' view of human nature not only as naive but also as seriously misguided because it fails to do justice to the unconscious which, for the analytical practitioner, largely determines an individual's behaviour and perception of reality.

The behavioural tradition tends to regard all hypotheses about the inner workings of the human being as largely irrelevant. For the convinced behaviourist they must for ever remain hypotheses in so far as they can never be adequately researched and tested. Quite simply it is not possible to prove the existence of the Freudian unconscious or of Rogers' internal locus of evaluation any more than it is possible to prove the existence of God. In the circumstances the behaviourist opts to understand human beings in terms of genetic structure and, more significantly, of environmental variables. He rejects the notion that behaviour arises from some source within the human being and prefers instead to see an individual's behaviour, including his or her thoughts and feelings, as primarily determined by environmental history and the present circumstances of the person's life. In some ways the behaviourist can appreciate the force of Rogers' emphasis on the central importance for human development of the core conditions because this is to speak in terms of a reinforcing environment which determines the individual's behavioural direction. The behaviourist parts company with Rogers, however, once the emphasis changes to an endorsement of the subjective life of the individual and to the fundamental significance of the internal locus of evaluation. This essential conflict is revealed in the famous dialogue between Rogers and the doyen of behaviourists, B.F. Skinner, which took place in 1962 and which has only recently seen publication in *Carl Rogers: Dialogues* (Kirschenbaum and Henderson, 1990b). At one point in this dialogue Skinner remarks:

> I always come back to the discovery that when I give up trying to account for something with an inner entity of some sort and try, very awkwardly at first, to deal with external entities which might be responsible for it, in the long run it comes out.

A few minutes later Rogers responds:

> In your talking about the external causes of behaviour, you spoke as though for every external cause we can find, then you can drop a previous erroneous internal cause which you formerly posited. . . . Yet one lives a subjective life as well as being a sequence of cause and effect. It seems to me this has an importance which you don't always acknowledge. (Kirschenbaum and Henderson, 1990b: 97-9)

The difference in theoretical standpoint could scarcely be clearer and the implications for therapeutic practice are enormous. For the behaviourist, Rogers' confidence in the individual's capacity to discover his or her own internal resources and wisdom is to fly in the face of the fact that we are all subject to external forces and conditions which must be controlled and manipulated so that we can be provided with opportunities for acquiring alternative behaviour to replace and extinguish the maladaptive patterns that spoil our lives.

Rogers' religious and theological critics are numerous, even if they are seldom united in their objections to his theories and practice. Most are agreed, however, that his understanding of human nature is at best defective and at worst erroneous. If, for the behaviourist, the notion of the internal locus of evaluation is an untestable hypothesis, for some theologians it smacks of a godless universe where the isolated conscious self becomes the sole judge of what the self should value and how it should behave. Rogers' human being is a creature without a sense of his or her creator and, as such, is woefully ill equipped for the challenges of life and for the encounter with death. Rogers' view of the individual is seen as selling human beings short by divorcing them from higher sources of wisdom and energy and from the religious and spiritual traditions that seek to give access to those sources. Critics of this persuasion see in Rogers' understanding of human nature a profoundly narcissistic tendency whereby the individual becomes the only arbiter and evaluator of his or her own conduct and experience. Without the concept of God or of a higher spiritual authority the individual is totally at the mercy of self-delusion and is likely to succumb to the cult of self-worship. One of the most virulent attacks on Rogers' view of human nature is contained in Paul Vitz's *Psychology as Religion* which has as its subtitle the very words 'the cult of self-worship' (Vitz, 1977). Vitz, a Christian professor of psychology, argues with great passion that humanistic psychologists in general and Rogers in particular have evolved a theory of human nature which inevitably leads to psychology itself becoming a religion in the form of a secular humanism based on worship of the self.

For many Christian apologists the inadequacy of Rogers' view of human nature resides not so much in its rejection of God as the source of all being but in its refusal to acknowledge the ravages of Original Sin. For these critics such blindness is as baffling as Rogers' apparent neglect of the unconscious is for the analyst. To the Christian, reared on the doctrinal tradition of the Fall–Redemption theology originating in St Augustine and alive and well today, it is inconceivable that anyone could be so wilfully obtuse as to regard human nature as essentially good and forward moving; such a perception of humanity is dangerous for it suggests that men and women have no need of redemption, that they do not require a saviour and that the death and resurrection of Christ are without meaning or significance. For such Christian critics Rogers' view of human nature strikes at the very heart of their understanding of the Christian gospel and, as such, ranks as a major heresy to be eradicated at the earliest opportunity. It is not only the understanding of human nature which is at stake, for Rogers' reluctance to acknowledge the fundamental defect in human beings and their built-in tendency to corruption brings into question the whole issue of evil in the world and in the cosmos. Nothing pleases the devil so much, such critics would argue, as the assumption that he does not exist.

Criticisms of Therapeutic Practice

In 1957 Carl Rogers met in public dialogue with the famous Jewish scholar and philosopher, Martin Buber. Buber's great contribution to the understanding of human development lies in his conviction that men and women are essentially relational creatures. In his celebrated *I and Thou* (1937) he enshrined his major thesis that 'life is meeting' and that salvation lies in glorifying neither the individual nor the collective but in the open dialogue of relationship. That Buber should debate with Rogers was wholly appropriate, for Rogers is often portrayed as the therapist who more than any other stresses the quality of relating between therapist and client as the primary source of healing. The dialogue that took place between the two men is notable on many scores and is of particular relevance for our present purposes because it ended with Buber clearly unconvinced about the nature of the relationship which Rogers experienced with his clients (Kirschenbaum and Henderson, 1990b: 63). Indeed, in the closing minutes of the dialogue, Buber implies that the therapeutic relationship resulting from client-centred therapy may produce individuals rather than persons, and he roundly declares himself to be against individuals and for persons. An individual, he explains, 'may become more and more an individual without making him more and more human. I have a lot of examples of man having become very very individual, very distinct of others, very developed in their such-and-such-ness without being at all what I would like to call a man.' Buber arrives at this disturbing reservation about the therapeutic practice which Rogers has sought to explain and explore in their conversation because he is unconvinced about the reciprocity of the therapeutic relationship. 'You are not equals and cannot be,' he says at one point and in these concise words he throws doubt on two issues central to Rogers' viewpoint. In the first place, he questions the power base of the therapeutic relationship and secondly he raises grave reservations about the individual's process of becoming if that process is not firmly anchored in what he calls 'real reciprocity' (Kirschenbaum and Henderson, 1990b: 50–63). Many of the criticisms which have been directed at Rogers' way of 'doing therapy' can be traced back to one or other of these central issues. The behaviour of the therapist, it is suggested, can create a situation where the client experiences confusion rather than empowerment, which then leads not to increasing autonomy but to a dependency on the therapist whose very acceptance and empathy leave the client without reference points of any kind. Furthermore, as the client becomes more in touch with powerful but repressed feelings he or she may develop a concept of self which, as it grows in strength and uniqueness, may feed a sense of alienation rather than of belongingness if the therapist is unable to safeguard the client's experience of connectedness.

The trust that the therapist places in the client leads to the attentive empathic listening which frequently characterizes much of client-centred therapy. When this is allied to a deep acceptance of the client there can be little doubt that for the vast majority of clients the therapist becomes unique in his or her experience. Nobody else in the client's life, it can safely be assumed, listens and accepts with such dedicated commitment and intensity. For the client this may be liberating and validating but it is also possible for the experience to be unnerving. The client is placed in a position where his or her words are accepted at face value and where the therapist apparently does not believe it necessary or even relevant to express an opinion about the rightness or wrongness of what is expressed. Harry Van Belle has suggested that for many clients this response may well seem mystifying in the extreme – precisely because it is so unlike their experience with other people in their lives (Van Belle, 1980: 148). They may conclude that the therapist sees them in a way that they cannot fathom and that, in this sense, the therapist is 'up to something' which is unknown to them. Van Belle comments that in such a situation the client may have no option but to trust the therapist totally on the assumption that the therapist at least knows what he or she is doing even if the client knows neither who he is nor what he should be doing! In an ironical way the therapist's trust in the client which finds expression in attentive listening, empathic understanding and deep acceptance leads not to the client trusting himself but to a total trust in the therapist. Far from empowering the client, Van Belle is suggesting that the therapist's response may induce a massive dependency which springs from the confusion at being received in so singular a fashion. This is another sign of the lack of reciprocity to which Buber draws attention in the dialogue and about which he clearly felt so uneasy. For Buber there is an imbalance in the relationship which deprives it of the creativity that is the hallmark of the true I – Thou dialogue, whereas for Van Belle it is the very operation of empathy and acceptance that can leave all the power with the therapist despite, perhaps, his sincere intention to empower the client.

These are serious criticisms for they strike at the heart of Rogers' beliefs. He attaches great importance to not interfering in the life of the client and to facilitating the process of the client's growth rather than directing it. He refrains from diagnosis and from interpretation in any traditional sense. Indeed, as Van Belle points out, such behaviours are regarded as antitherapeutic (Van Belle, 1980: 146). And yet the very absence of such feedback may serve to prolong and even exacerbate the power imbalance which it is Rogers' avowed aim to eradicate.

More serious still, perhaps, is the implication of Rogers' acceptance at face value of what clients say. Nye, amongst others, has questioned the adequacy of a therapeutic method that relies on data obtained simply by listening empathically to those who seek help (Nye, 1986: 150). He refers to the large body of psychological evidence which indicates that it is often very difficult for a person to be understood let alone to express adequately 'real' feelings or thoughts. When to this difficulty is added the possibility that conscious, let alone unconscious, distortions may be present in client statements then it becomes even more questionable whether a satisfactorily complete picture of individuals can be obtained simply by listening to them. The accusation can readily be levelled that Rogers' methodology is the inevitable outcome of his phenomenology and that both are equally naive.

Buber's uncomfortableness about the evolution of individuals rather than persons points to the most serious criticism of all as far as Rogers' view of therapeutic process is concerned for, if it has substance, the whole theoretical edifice of Rogers' work is endangered. Buber implies that it is possible for an individual to achieve an increasingly strong sense of his or her own unique identity without a corresponding awareness of others and without the development of the responsiveness which makes for social responsibility. Rogers, on the other hand, repeatedly affirmed his belief that men and women are essentially social creatures and that, given the opportunity to experience their own value, they will inevitably develop in a way which is socially constructive. Buber's scepticism about this optimistic viewpoint closely mirrors the Christian objection that Rogers fails to acknowledge humanity's basic tendency to evil. In terms of therapeutic process this theme is strongly revisited in an 'Open Letter' which Rollo May addressed to Rogers in 1982 through the pages of the *Journal of Humanistic Psychology*. In this letter May refers to the Wisconsin experiment, which Rogers and his colleagues had conducted with schizophrenic patients twenty years earlier, and to his own experience of listening to tapes of the therapy conducted at that time. He comments:

> After listening to the tapes you sent me, I reported that, while I felt the therapy was good on the whole, there was one glaring omission. This was that the client-centered therapists did not (or could not) deal with the angry, hostile, negative – that is, evil – feelings of the client.

Later in the same letter, he goes on to say:

> The issue of evil – or rather the issue of not confronting evil – has profound, and to my mind, adverse effects on humanistic psychology. I believe it is the most important error in the humanistic movement. (May, 1982: 10–21)

The combined criticisms of Buber and May cast doubt on the 'realness' of the therapeutic relationship in client-centred therapy in so far as it may lack genuine reciprocity, and on the capacity of client-centred therapists, because of their belief system, to acknowledge and confront the evil and destructive tendencies in their clients. The very mode of therapy, it is suggested, can encourage the development of a narcissistic individualism based on a misplaced self-love which evades the confrontation with the negative. In short, the process induced by client-centred therapy is not trustworthy. Van Belle, in his mainly sympathetic book on Rogers (Van Belle, 1980), adds further fuel to the critical fire by calling into question not only the validity of the therapeutic process as Rogers describes it but also the emphasis in Rogers' work as a whole on process and changingness.

Van Belle notes that in Rogers' concept of the fully functioning person it is the quality of changingness which merits the highest accolade; indeed for Rogers the fully functioning person is the 'epitome of man as a process'. Van Belle is troubled by this notion and sees in it the danger that men and women could be tied to a life of excessive change and could thereby lose all sense of a solid identity. Once more there seems to be the lurking danger of confusion, disorientation and a lack of anchorage. Van Belle is equally unhappy about Rogers' conviction that the process of therapy itself will follow an inevitable path. He questions whether the client's open expression of feelings and their empathic and acceptant reception by the therapist will automatically be followed by insight and cognitive clarification and he is equally uncertain whether this phase will be followed by the client's capacity to act upon his insights. Van Belle's doubt about the inevitability of the therapeutic process is great enough for him to question Rogers' fundamental belief that the therapist has only to be the facilitator, the companion of the client, for the process to occur. In the closing pages of his book Van Belle goes so far as to reject the notion of therapy as a facilitative event and with it the belief that the therapeutic process can occur spontaneously in the client once the core conditions have been established. He argues that the process, if it is to occur, needs the aid of the therapist's intervention every step of the way and that therapy must be a *co-operative* activity. Indeed, it is difficult to avoid the conclusion that Van Belle, after painstakingly exploring Rogers' theoretical beliefs and clinical practice with consummate accuracy and sensitivity, proceeds in the final quarter of his book partially to demolish the elegant edifice which he has illuminated (Van Belle, 1980: 145–55).

It would be impossible to consider criticisms of Rogers' therapeutic practice without drawing attention to one issue that has continually attracted debate and not infrequently led to heated differences of opinion. For analytical practitioners the concept of the transference is central to the understanding of therapeutic process and the 'working through' of the transference is often seen as fundamental to the successful outcome of therapy. In such 'working through' clients have the chance to re-experience earlier relationships as they 'transfer' past emotions on to the therapist. In doing this they may experience the therapist by turn as positive, demanding, even rejecting and, as the process develops, the therapist must take great care to guard against countertransference, which is an inappropriate emotional reaction to the client, and to remain objective in the face of what can at times be a bewildering array of emotions. Because of Rogers' inadequate attention to unconscious forces, as the analyst sees it, the whole transference–countertransference dynamic is missing from client-centred therapy, at least in any overt way. The analytical criticism, however, revolves around the belief that transference takes place *whether the therapist acknowledges this or not* and that Rogers, by his failure to give due respect to this unconscious dimension, is in danger of attributing to the relationship which he forms with his clients a quality of present reality that cannot be sustained. Rogers himself was never tempted into lengthy dispute about this contentious issue but because the concept of transference is so widespread and still seems to have such a powerful grip on the therapeutic professions and even on many members of the public, it cannot be ignored in a survey of critical responses to Rogers' way of 'doing therapy'.

The Case of Jeffrey Masson

In 1989, in his book *Against Therapy*, Jeffrey Masson, former analyst and projects director of the Sigmund Freud archives, launched an extraordinary attack on the very foundations of modern psychotherapy. His disenchantment with psychoanalysis had set in much earlier with his attack in *The Assault on Truth* (1984) on Freud's suppression of the seduction theory but the 1989 book casts its net of condemnation much wider. Masson's thesis is that abuse of one kind or another is built into the very fabric of psychotherapy because it is of the nature of psychotherapy to distort another person's reality. Much of Masson's book is taken up with a devastating exploration of various figures in the history of analysis and he reserves his most violent attack for the discredited John Rosen, the initiator of so-called 'direct psychoanalysis'. There is a chapter on sex and battering in psychotherapy where Masson assembles overwhelming evidence of physical and sexual abuse of a most extreme kind. Immediately following this chapter Masson turns his attention to a therapist who, by universal recognition, he acknowledges to be 'kind, compassionate, helpful'. This is Carl Rogers, who comes under Masson's condemnatory searchlight to be shown as a benevolent despot whose practice is built on the same bedrock as that of the manifest abusers Masson has already exposed so ruthlessly.

Masson seeks to demonstrate that there can be no real genuineness in the relationships offered by a client-centred therapist because it is only the artificiality of the therapy situation which enables the therapist to 'play out' the core conditions for brief periods of time. Nobody, Masson argues, could ever in 'real life' do the things Rogers prescribes that the therapist should do. 'If the therapist manages to do so in a session, if he appears to be all-accepting and all-understanding, this is merely artifice; it is not reality.' Masson goes on to accuse Rogers of complete indifference to the glaring injustices suffered by many clients as a result of societal and other forces. In a powerful analysis of Rogers' Wisconsin research project on hospitalized schizophrenics he shows Rogers to have been callously indifferent to the abusive practices of psychiatry and condemns him for having closed his eyes to the evident injustices and humiliations which many of the patients endured. Indeed, he berates Rogers for having colluded with the hospital administration in order to further his own professional interests and that of the research project. In a final section, Masson turns his attention to the practice of empathic responsiveness and to Rogers' determination not to make interpretations of his clients' statements. He praises Rogers for his genuine desire not to intrude on the thought processes of his clients but concludes that this is simply not possible: 'There is no way out of this dilemma. It is in the nature of therapy to distort another person's reality' (Masson, 1989: 229–47).

Masson's attack on Rogers must be seen in the context of his impassioned onslaught on the whole practice and profession of psychotherapy but in its specific criticisms it reverberates with other opinions rehearsed in this chapter. His cynical view of the artificial nature of the therapeutic relationship is a much more extreme expression of the doubts expressed by Buber. The lack of attention to the realities of social injustice and the abuse of medical power is further ammunition for the behaviourist point of view which sees Rogers as seriously deficient in his evaluation of external forces. The impossibility of offering an empathic understanding which does not distort the client's reality belongs to the same category of criticism as Van Belle's questioning of the empowerment of clients through empathy and acceptance. The force of Masson's attack lies, however, in his acknowledgement of Rogers' benevolence. The benevolent despot is seen as a figure who is just as sinister as his malevolent counterpart, for he exercises power covertly. In Rogers' case, Masson would argue that the abuse of power is concealed by the claim that the very reverse is happening. The therapist who professes to be relinquishing power so that his client may be empowered is, in reality, intervening in the life of another person with powerful and manipulative intent.

Research Critique
In their introduction to *Client-Centered Therapy and the Person-Centered Approach* (Levant and Shlien, 1984), the editors point to the troubling situation in the area of research into client-centred therapy. They show that until the mid-1970s there was considerable support for Rogers' hypotheses regarding the necessary and sufficient conditions for psychotherapy or at least for the clear connection of the facilitative conditions with therapeutic outcome. This favourable conclusion was, however, much in dispute by the end of the 1970s as researchers from traditions other than the client-centred conducted studies and as other workers exposed faulty research design in previous studies. Levant and Shlien conclude that as far as client-centred therapy is concerned neither research methodology nor outcome evaluation have much to be proud of. This gloomy summary somewhat undermines the previous security expressed by many client-centred therapists as a result of the knowledge that their approach was one of the best researched in the whole field of psychotherapy.

Later in the book, however, Neill Watson in a detailed review of a large number of research studies presents a further reflection. He concludes that in his review he located no studies that adequately tested Rogers' hypotheses. Most particularly, he draws attention to the fact that a large number of studies have used judge ratings of the therapist-provided conditions to the total neglect of client perceptions of the relationship, which are essential to a test of the hypotheses. Where studies *have* explored client perceptions of the relationship they have typically not included all the hypothesized conditions and have therefore failed to take account of the fact that Rogers' propositions address a *set* of necessary and sufficient conditions. Watson ends his review: 'After twenty-five years of research on Rogers' hypotheses, there is not yet research of the rigor required for drawing conclusions about the validity of this important theory' (Watson, 1984: 40).

It is intriguing, to say the least, that Watson's review reveals the difficulty that researchers have apparently experienced in giving the primacy to the client's perception of what is going on in the therapeutic process. The reliance on 'expert' external judges makes nonsense of Rogers' hypotheses and yet it appears that such research has been carried out in good faith, sometimes at Rogers' own instigation, without awareness of its irrelevance to the testing of the hypotheses. Those who criticize the research on client-centred therapy for its inadequacy or inconclusiveness are justified, but it is worth recalling again that towards the end of his life Rogers was increasingly aware of the need for new research paradigms if the phenomenological world of the client was to become the cornerstone of research in the same way that it is central to the therapeutic endeavour of the client-centred therapist.

Summary of Criticisms

Many of the criticisms which have been levelled against Rogers and his work have their origin in what his critics see as his grossly inflated trust in and regard for the individual. Such a view threatens those whose professional identity is closely bound up with the importance of their psychological expertise and knowledge in the healing of others: Rogers reinforced such anxiety by his deep ambivalence towards institutions of all kinds, by his own distrust of authority and by his conviction that nothing of significance could ever be taught. The only learning that significantly influences behaviour, he believed, is self-discovered learning.

His view of human nature has proved unacceptable to a wide variety of critics. For the analysts and for many Christian commentators he not only has too optimistic a perception of human potential but also greatly underrates the forces of the unconscious and of evil. For the behaviourists his belief in the subjective core of the human personality is an unprovable hypothesis which blinds him to the overriding influence of environmental conditions and behavioural reinforcements. For all these critics, Rogers' notion of the internalized locus of evaluation as a kind of innate mechanism which is trustworthy remains unconvincing and unpersuasive.

Rogers' therapeutic practice has been criticized on many scores but among the more serious criticisms is the doubt cast on the effectiveness of the relationships created by client-centred therapists to develop a socially responsive attitude in clients. It has also been argued, by Van Belle, that the belief in the core conditions as facilitating client autonomy may be misplaced and that the experience of intensive empathy and acceptance may actually engender a deep dependency on the therapist. Van Belle has cast doubt, too, on the notion of therapy as simply facilitative and has questioned the inevitability of the therapeutic process as Rogers describes it. The validity of the therapeutic relationship in client-centred therapy is deeply suspect in the eyes of many analytical practitioners, who see Rogers' neglect of transference processes as an omission with far-reaching consequences.

Jeffrey Masson's ferocious attack on psychotherapy in general and on Rogers as the seductive example of the benevolent despot draws together in accentuated and radical form many of the threads of opposition discernible in other writers. The force of Masson's critique lies in its contention that Rogers' very benevolence obscures the essential abuse of power which characterizes his therapeutic practice.

The considerable body of research into client-centred therapy has been shown by recent reviews to be seriously flawed in many respects. The proud boast that Rogers was wont to make that client-centred therapy was well supported by empirical research (much of it instigated by himself and his associates) is now shown to be less than convincing. Indeed, it would seem that, as yet, Rogers' own hypotheses as he originally formulated them, remain untested.

Rebuttals

Contemporary Relevance
The market-place mentality and the desire for quick solutions at financially affordable prices are aspects of only one dimension of contemporary western society, albeit an overtly dominant one. Nor does the search for experts and instant gurus reflect the whole

picture. There is plenty of evidence to suggest that we are living at a time when disenchantment with political systems of all kinds is widespread and where materialism, both economically and philosophically, is showing signs of incipient collapse. The re-emergence of political conservatism and even of pockets of fundamentalist Christianity both in America and Europe are a somewhat desperate if determined attempt to put the clock back to an era where authority structures were for the most part unquestioned and unchallenged. It is not necessary to be a social analyst to observe that in most western cultures the movement towards greater personal consciousness is well-nigh universal.

Recent events in the former Soviet Union mark an increasing acceleration of this astonishing process. In Britain the development of counselling and therapy during the past decade indicates an important sea-change: it is now culturally acceptable to seek help for emotional and psychological concerns. In such a changing context Rogers and his ideas find a ready audience: his validation of subjective experience and his emphasis on the facilitative relationship appeal greatly to a generation which has little faith in dogmatic rigidity of any kind and which often pines for intimacy and meaning in personal relationships. It may be that Rogers and client-centred therapy are looked at askance in academia and in some professional circles but in countless self-help groups, in counselling skills courses in colleges, churches and evening institutes, in human relations programmes within educational and institutional settings, it will more often than not be the work of Rogers which underpins the enterprise. Rogers' confidence in the individual person and his commitment to the development of personal power draw a ready response from those innumerable individuals who find in his work a path to greater self-awareness and deeper relationship. Rogers may be out of tune with the technological market-place and its frenetic search for psychological magic but he is assuredly a principal source of inspiration for those who are already disenchanted with mechanistic views of reality and sense that new paradigms must soon be embraced if society is to move away from the brink of disaster.

Human Nature

To those critics who accused him of having too optimistic a view of human nature, Rogers always gave essentially the same answer. He pointed to his own experience as a therapist and called upon the evidence. Thus it is that in an article in 1957 he writes:

My views of man's most basic characteristics have been formed by my experience in psychotherapy. They include certain observations as to what man is *not*, as well as some description of what, in my experience, he *is*. Let me state these very briefly. . . .

I do not discover man to be well characterized in his basic nature by such terms as *fundamentally hostile, antisocial, destructive, evil*.

I do not discover man to be, in his basic nature, completely without a nature, a tabula rasa on which anything may be written, nor malleable putty which can be shaped in any form.

I do not discover man to be essentially a perfect being, sadly warped and corrupted by society.

In my experience I have discovered man to have characteristics which seem inherent in his species, and the terms which have at different times seemed to me descriptive of these characteristics are such terms as *positive, forward-moving, constructive, realistic, trustworthy*. (Rogers, 1957b: 200)

In 1982 in a response to Rollo May's 'Open Letter' – and equally pertinent to the attack by the Christian critic, Paul Vitz – he wrote:

When you speak of the narcissism that has been fostered by humanistic psychology and how many individuals are 'lost in self love', I feel like speaking up and saying 'That's not true!'. . . In the groups with which I've had contact, the truth is quite the contrary. Such groups lead to social action of a realistic nature. Individuals who come in as social fanatics become much more socially realistic, but they still want to take action. People who have not been very aware of social issues become more aware and, again, opt for realistic actions on those issues. We have had plenty of evidence of this in our encounter groups and workshops. Irrational anger and violence are sometimes defused, but action of a more realistic sort increases. (Rogers, 1982: 85)

The issue of self-love is addressed again in Rogers' review of the book *The Self and the Dramas of History* by the theologian, Reinhold Niebuhr which appeared in 1956. Once more Rogers draws on his therapeutic experience, this time to refute Niebuhr's notion of Original Sin.

It is in his [Niebuhr's] conception of the basic deficiency of the individual self that I find my experience utterly at variance. He is quite clear that the 'original sin' is self love, pretension, claiming too much, grasping after self-realization. I read such words and try to imagine the experience out of which they have grown. I have dealt with maladjusted and troubled individuals, in the intimate personal relationship of psychotherapy, for more than a quarter of a century. This has not been perhaps a group fully representative of the whole community, but neither has it been unrepresentative. And, if I were to search for the central core of difficulty in people as I have come to know them, it is that in the great majority of cases they despise themselves, regard themselves as worthless and unlovable. . . . I could not differ more deeply from the notion that self love is the fundamental and pervasive 'sin'. (Rogers, 1956: 4)

Rogers' own experience of human beings constantly leaves him baffled by the propositions of theologians and psychologists alike. In the 1957 article referred to above he confesses himself bewildered by the statement of the Freudian, Karl Menninger, that he perceives man as 'innately evil' or 'innately destructive'. Rogers asks himself how it could be that Menninger and he, working with such similar purposes in intimate therapeutic relationships, could come to view people so differently. He even goes so far as to advance hypotheses as to the reasons for the wide discrepancy between the Freudian view of man's nature and his own. Interestingly, he suggests that because Freud relied on self-analysis he was deprived of the warmly acceptant relationship which is necessary if apparently destructive and negative aspects of the self are ever to be accepted fully as having meaning and a constructive part to play.

Rogers' deep and lasting trust in human nature did not blind him to the reality of evil *behaviour*. In his discussion of Niebuhr's book he refutes the notion that he is an optimist. 'It disturbs me,' he writes, 'to be thought of as an optimist. My whole professional experience has been with the dark and often sordid side of life, and I know, better than most, the incredibly destructive behaviour of which man is capable. Yet that same professional experience has forced upon me the realization that man, when you know him deeply, in his worst and most troubled states, is not evil or demonic' (Rogers, 1958: 17). In his reply to Rollo May he writes in similar vein:

> In my experience, every person has the capacity for evil behaviour. I, and others, have had murderous and cruel impulses, desires to hurt, feelings of anger and rage, desires to impose our wills on others. . . . Whether I, or any one, will translate these impulses into behaviour depends, it seems to me, on two elements: social conditioning and voluntary choice. . . . I believe that, theoretically at least, every evil behaviour is brought about by varying degrees of these elements. (Rogers, 1982: 88)

There is evidence that Rogers was not wholly satisfied with his own arguments in favour of man's essential trustworthiness despite the almost overwhelmingly positive data from his therapeutic experience. In the response to Rollo May he admits that he finds 'a shocking puzzle' in the famous experiments by Stanley Milgram and Philip Zimbardo which demonstrated, in the first case, that 60 per cent of people were willing to turn up electric current to a voltage which they knew would kill others and, in the second, that randomly assigned 'guards' and 'prisoners' were rapidly caught up in violent destructiveness which became life threatening.

Furthermore, in 1981 he contributed a leading article to the first number of the short-lived 'international notebook', *Journey*, in which he wrote:

> We are often asked, how do we account for evil or the dark side of human nature, the shadow side? How do we explain irrational violence and the rising crime rate etc? My own feeling is that we have an answer to this question, but I am not sure that it is an adequate answer. (Rogers, 1981: 1)

Adequate answer or not, Rogers did not deviate from his belief in the positive and trustworthy basis of human nature and continued through the years to give the primacy to his own experience as a therapist. He seems to have been ignorant of theological traditions that might well have buttressed his own deeply held convictions. His family background together with the attacks made upon him by Christian writers steeped in the Augustinian notion of Original Sin meant that to the end of his life he saw Christianity as essentially hostile to human nature and caught up in guilt-inducing judgementalism. In recent years, however, the more ancient spiritual tradition of original righteousness and original blessing is being rediscovered in the Christian church and with it the hopefulness for human evolution which is characteristic of Rogers' viewpoint. Such hopefulness is not to be confused with optimism for, like Rogers, theologians of this tradition are too much in touch with the pain and tragedy of human existence for that (for example Allchin, 1988). Nonetheless the doctrines of original righteousness and deification proclaim a humanity that is made in God's image and that men and women are partakers of the divine nature and are made for union with God. Such doctrines have inspired those Christians down the ages who have seen the glory of men and women as lying in their capacity to realize their divine potential through their relationship both with God and with each other. Theologians of this school of thought would agree with Rogers that, far from being caught up in the grandiosity of self-love, most human beings are trapped by feelings of worthlessness and self-contempt. It is only by recognizing and escaping from the deeply damaging effects of such self-denigration that they come into their divine inheritance. In brief, such a theology enshrines belief in a God who is unconditionally accepting and bears no resemblance to the judgemental figure of Rogers' youth and the theological tradition which he came so much to detest. The 'creation-centred' tradition, as it is often known, offers a view of the divine nature and of the evolving cosmos which is wholly supportive of Rogers' understanding of human beings and of their capacity for growth once they have internalized the liberating truth that they are un-conditionally accepted.

Rogers' admission that he was not convinced that his answer to the problem of evil was an adequate one together with his response to Rollo May that evil behaviour springs from varying degrees of 'social conditioning and voluntary choice' together constitute a humble but powerful response to both the behavioural and analytical viewpoints. It is the essence of the phenomenological position, when carried to its logical conclusion, that the human organism is unknowable in scientific terms. Because of the primacy given to subjectivity, each individual, according to Rogers, lives in a private world of experience which he or she alone has the capacity to understand. Not even the most empathic and sensitive therapist can fully understand another person. Rogers' tentativeness and deep respect for mystery makes it impossible for him to accept either the determinism of behaviouristic psychology or the complex theories of the unconscious advanced by the analytical schools. In response to the behaviourists he acknowledges the power of social conditioning and indeed much of his own understanding of human development is based on the adverse effects of the conditions of worth imposed by others. At the same time, however, it is impossi-ble for him to deny the reality and the importance of human choice. From his experience in therapy he has observed individuals struggling to develop and wrestling with decisions which ultimately they have made. To this extent he has seen people being the architects of their own lives. Once more it is his *experience* of intimate relating to others which compels him to reject the absolutism of the behavioural position.

The same experience prevents him from embracing any of the maps of the unconscious, for it is clear that we are all to some extent influenced by forces outside our awareness. Far from pleading guilty to the charge that he ignores the unconscious, Rogers would assuredly claim that his respect for the unconscious compels him to refrain from adopting any map of this essentially unknowable terrain which might lead him to impose his view or interpretation upon his client. In short, Rogers accepts both the reality of social conditioning and of the unconscious but refrains from elevating either to a position where they threaten to deprive individuals of the freedom to trust their own subjective experience and the mystery of their own natures.

Therapeutic Practice

Many of the criticisms of Rogers' therapeutic practice, as we have seen, revolve around the unreality of the relationship which is created between therapist and client. Buber complained about the lack of true reciprocity and was unconvinced by Rogers' contention that a meeting or dialogue can take place purely within the experiential world of the client. For Buber the life-giving 'I–Thou' relationship is only possible when both frames of reference are experienced simultaneously. Egocentricity is thereby transcended as both partners in a relationship experience themselves in the other person's skin without losing contact with their own realities. May accuses Rogers and his colleagues of failing to cope effectively with negative feelings in their clients, Van Belle questions the efficacy of empathy and acceptance in encouraging client autonomy while Masson dismisses the whole therapeutic enterprise as grotesquely inauthentic and inevitably manipulative.

Rogers in his reply to May makes an admission which has considerable relevance to this discussion. Commenting on May's judgement that client-centred therapists fail to accept and respond to negative feelings in general he says: 'I think that to some extent this was definitely true of me in the distant past.' He goes on to describe the changes in himself over the years and refers to both films and published transcripts which demonstrate his growing ability to handle negative and hostile reactions. He concludes: 'I believe I have learned to be acceptant of anger toward me and toward others' (Rogers, 1982: 86).

It can be seen from these brief comments that Rogers himself believed that his therapeutic style had changed over time, and this is supported by researchers who have studied his work in the years since his death (for example Van Balen, 1990; Temaner Brodley, 1991). Although these studies show no change in Rogers' dedication to discovering the perceptual world of the client, they do indicate a shift in his willingness to give a more personal expression of himself in his interaction with his clients.

Van Balen in his study sees the dialogue with Buber as having a decisive influence on Rogers' practice and quotes Rogers himself, writing in 1974, in support of this thesis:

> This recognition of the significance of what Buber terms the I–Thou relationship is the reason why, in client-centred therapy, there has come to be a greater use of the self of the therapist, of the therapist's feelings, a greater stress on genuineness, but all of this without imposing the views, values or interpretations of the therapist on the client. (Rogers, 1974b: 11)

Van Balen and others are also agreed that the 'Wisconsin project' with schizophrenic patients, despite May's reservations, actually gave rise to an increased emphasis on the therapist's use of his own thoughts and feelings in order to establish contact with persons who might themselves be very uncommunicative or even completely silent. It seems that this project together with the intensive group experiences in which Rogers was later to participate gradually led him to the point where he could state unequivocally that genuineness or congruence was the most basic of the conditions that foster therapeutic growth.

This movement towards greater authenticity and appropriate self-revelation is, I believe, the most powerful reply to those who accuse Rogers of creating one-sided relationships which are essentially manipulative or which encourage an unanchored narcissism. Through his increasing emphasis on the congruence of the therapist Rogers acknowledges that self-revelation, without imposition, can help to bring about the reciprocity of relationship which engenders mutual respect and avoids the dangers of confused dependence which Van Belle sees as a possible outcome of undiluted acceptance and empathy. There is a particular irony in the notion that the Wisconsin project played a crucial part in this move towards what Van Balen has called 'authenticity as an independent pole of interaction', for one of the other commonly held criticisms of client-centred therapy is that it is useful for articulate neurotics but of little value in the treatment of mentally ill individuals. It would seem that Rogers in his work with the Wisconsin patients not only demonstrated the validity of client-centred therapy with those suffering from so-called psychosis but also gave a new impetus to the practice of his approach. Increasingly 'being open to the other' became a significant goal for both therapist and client and was seen to be related to the client's achievement of self-acceptance as a consequence of feeling accepted. Perhaps acceptance of this life-transforming kind can only be experienced at the hands of a person whose own reality and vulnerability are readily accessible: an acceptant, empathic mirror or *alter ego* is not enough.

Jeffrey Masson's depiction of Rogers as a man indifferent to the abuses of the psychiatric system and blind to political realities scarcely seems just in the light of Rogers' lifelong struggle with the psychiatric 'establishment' and his deep and energetic commitment to world peace in his final years. Most people, after all, would have been content to relax into a well-merited retirement. Masson's basic premiss that it is the nature of therapy to distort another person's reality is more difficult to refute for unless a therapist is a perfect mirror – and hence a frustrating bore for his or her clients – there must be a sense in which the therapist interacts with the client's reality and to that extent changes or modifies it. Masson's argument is that this is what we do all the time in our social relationships and that it is therefore dishonest and deceitful for Rogers to suggest that he does not. I am not sure that Rogers ever claims to be so totally non-intrusive but it is certainly the case that in many of his writings he presents the therapist as solely the facilitator of the client's process which, once the core conditions have been established, unfolds spontaneously and inevitably. When Van Belle argues that this concept of facilitation is an erroneous analysis of the therapist's role he seems to be joining with Masson in accusing Rogers of a certain level of self-deception. Such criticism loses some of its force, however, if we believe all human life to be essentially relational. In this sense – and here again Buber's position is relevant – we need the other for our own completion. My reality needs the other's response if it is to be complete, and distortion comes not through the response in itself which is essential to the integrity of my reality but through a lack of respect for and understanding of my inner world. To accept Masson's critique of therapy as a distorting activity is tantamount to writing off all human relationships as destructive of the individual's subjective reality. Masson, it seems, would prefer us to be isolated creatures who steer clear of human interaction in the interests of preserving our perceptual purity. This seems conducive to madness because it is a denial of our need for relationship if we are to establish a sense of self.

Van Belle's rejection of facilitation in favour of co-operation as the essential task of the therapist is one with which I have considerable sympathy. I also believe it to be in keeping with the behaviour of the later Rogers for whom the capacity to be congruent assumes increasing importance. Barbara Temaner Brodley, in her recent study of Rogers' verbal behaviour in therapy sessions, states of his latest period (1977–86) that Rogers' responses from his own point of view increased from 4 to 16 per cent over the previous period (1944–64). Interestingly most of the increase appears in the categories of therapist's comments, interpretations and explanations. She notes, too, that Rogers in these closing years was slightly more inclined to voice agreement with his clients and to pose leading questions (Temaner Brodley, 1991: 13). It appears that Rogers through his manifest behaviour had come close to accepting the validity of Van Belle's point of view that the therapeutic process requires the active participation of the therapist all the way. Therapy is a co-operative event achieved by the client and the therapist working together (Van Belle, 1980: 150).

In 1984 John Shlien, one of Rogers' earliest students and an Emeritus Professor at Harvard, published a startling paper entitled 'A countertheory of transference'. It begins with the provocative statement: 'Transference is a fiction, invented and maintained by the therapist to protect himself from the consequences of his own behaviour' (Shlien, 1984: 153). The paper caused considerable debate and some three years later an edition of the *Person-Centered Review* was largely devoted to responses and reactions to Shlien's ideas from a number of eminent therapists of different therapeutic traditions. Rogers contributed to this symposium but by the time it was published in May 1987 he had died, at the age of 85. There is something poignant about the fact that the issue of transference should have been the subject of Rogers' last theoretical paper for, despite the controversial nature of the subject, he had not previously chosen to enter into combat on the issue.

In the *Review* article, Rogers begins by welcoming Shlien's paper as competent, timely and important. He also declares himself to be in agreement with its major thesis and is particularly delighted that it should have come from the pen of a man who was 'an enthusiastic student of Freudian analysis' before he became a client-centred practitioner. Here Rogers is relishing the opportunity to express his support for Shlien and it is not surprising that what follows contains much scarcely concealed hostility towards analytical orthodoxy. After first discussing client feelings that are an understandable response to the therapist's attitudes and behaviour, Rogers embarks upon his discussion of client reactions which are 'the emotions that have little or no relationship to the therapist's behaviour'. Such emotions he describes as truly 'transferred' from their real origin to the therapist and he labels them projections which may be positive feelings of love, sexual desire and the like or negative feelings of hatred, contempt, fear, distrust. He continues: 'Their true object may be a parent or other significant person in the client's life. Or, and this is less often recognised, they may be negative attitudes towards the self, which the client cannot bear to face.' The paragraph which follows is a clear expression of Rogers' view on how such feelings should be handled in a therapeutic relationship, and merits quoting in full:

> From a client-centered point of view, it is not necessary in responding to and dealing with these feelings, to determine whether they are therapist caused or are projections. The distinction is of theoretical interest, but is not a practical problem. In the therapeutic interaction all of these attitudes – positive or negative, 'transference' feelings, or therapist-caused reactions – are best dealt with in the same way. If the therapist is sensitively understanding and genuinely acceptant and nonjudgmental, therapy will move forward through these feelings. There is absolutely no need to make a special case of attitudes that are transferred to the therapist and no need for the therapist to permit the dependence that is so often a part of other forms of therapy, particularly psychoanalysis. It is entirely possible to accept dependent feelings

without permitting the client to change the therapist's role. (Rogers, 1987: 183–4)

There then follows a case example previously published in *Client-Centered Therapy* in 1951 and the article concludes with some observations about psychoanalysis which show Rogers at his most militant and aggressive. Having once more made the point that *all* feelings directed towards the therapist should be dealt with by the creation of a therapeutic relationship characterized by the core conditions, he continues:

> To deal with transference feelings as a very special part of therapy, making their handling the very core of therapy, is to my mind a grave mistake. Such an approach fosters dependence and lengthens therapy. It creates a whole new problem, the only purpose of which appears to be the intellectual satisfaction of the therapist – showing the elaborateness of his or her expertise. I deplore it.

Even then Rogers has not finished and it seems as if his anger must find further expression. He challenges the analysts to present their data and provide evidence for their belief that the 'transference neurosis' is so important to successful therapy. Where, he asks, are the recorded interviews which would prove the point? The article ends with a challenge which, one suspects, Rogers knew was unlikely to be accepted. 'Why the reluctance to make known what actually happens in the therapist's dealings with this core of the analytic process?. . . The questions cannot be finally answered until psychoanalysts are willing to open their work to professional scrutiny' (Rogers, 1987: 187–8).

Research

It is difficult to accept that the formidable amount of research undertaken on client-centred therapy has been utterly in vain. Whilst it appears true that Rogers' original hypotheses remain untested because of faulty research design and a failure to explore the hypotheses as a complete package, there remains considerable support for the more modest assertion that the qualities of acceptance, empathy and congruence are at least connected with therapeutic effectiveness. Evidence for the potency of the facilitative conditions also comes from research in hundreds of classrooms both in the USA (Aspy and Roebuck, 1983) and in Germany (Tausch, 1978). Clearly, we still await the necessary conditions for evaluating client-centred therapy and it remains to be seen whether the eventual breakthrough will come through the more rigorous application of the 'objective' methods of yesteryear or through the development of new research paradigms more in harmony with the spirit of the phenomenological view of reality (Mearns and McLeod, 1984). What is certain is that researchers are once more wrestling with the complexity of the task in an attempt to revive Rogers' earlier commitment to a coherent integration of theory, practice and research.

Conclusion

Many people find in Rogers' writings a clear articulation of what they themselves have felt and thought confusedly for many years. Such people – and I count myself among them – respond instantly to a person who conveys powerfully what it involves to struggle towards self-acceptance and to discover a respect for one's own experience. Rogers' theoretical formulations also offer a way of relating to oneself and to others which is compelling in so far as it encourages honesty, openness, understanding and acceptant responsiveness. Rogers offers a way of being which is attractive and even seductive, for it gives absolute primacy to subjective reality and yet places this supreme value within the context of a mode of relating which promises a high level of intimacy.

Rogers' critics are for the most part resistant to such seduction. They are less inclined to attribute such overriding importance to subjective reality and doubt the capacity of human beings – even well-intentioned therapists – to embody the core conditions to the extent that Rogers advocates. They detect within Rogers' concern for the autonomy of the individual an ambiguity about the nature of the relationship which is being offered in therapy. At times the apparently self-effacing behaviour of the therapist suggests that, once the core conditions have been established, he or she only has to provide a particular psychological environment and the therapeutic process in the client will unfold spontaneously and inevitably. At other times Rogers appears to acknowledge the centrality of the therapist's own congruence and his or her willingness to be involved in a reciprocal exchange as long as there is no intention of imposing on the client's reality.

There was initially, I believe, a genuine confusion at the heart of Rogers' thinking and his critics in one way or another tend to sniff this out. Rogers never seemed to be absolutely sure whether men and women are essentially relational beings or not. His tendency to employ images culled from agriculture and his emphasis on the actualizing tendency and the wisdom of the organism can lead to a highly positive view of the human being but one which is strangely non-relational except that the evolution of the species is seen to be part of a universal formative tendency. Because of this central confusion Rogers' critics – rightly in my view – question the nature of the relationship between therapist and client and raise doubts about Rogers' view of therapy as essentially the facilitation of inherent growth processes. Rogers' constant emphasis upon process and changingness and his apparent preference for affective as opposed to cognitive experience have led some of his critics to accuse him of, at one and the same time, affirming the uniqueness of persons and denying them any continuing or stable identity.

For my own part, I acknowledge the inconsistencies and, at times, the logical contradictions in Rogers' point of view. I am reassured, however, by my powerful memories of the man himself. In my own relationship with him, I never for one moment feared that we would be lost in an infinite process of becoming. On the contrary, I recall many an encounter from which I gained a heightened sense of my own identity and a powerful impression of Rogers' complex but integrated personality. In practice, there was never for one moment any doubt that we were both unique and that our uniqueness was characterized by the fact that we were relational beings. Rogers' keen interest in everything around him and his capacity for drawing pleasure from his social environment provided ample evidence that he was well aware of the ways in which our social context can support personal development as well as impede it. For a man dedicated to the understanding of the subjective world of others he was wonderfully at home in the mundane world of eating, drinking and catching the next post.

5

The Overall Influence of Carl Rogers

An International Network

In July 1991 I returned from the Second International Conference on Client-Centred and Experiential Psychotherapy held in the University of Stirling, Scotland. The first such conference took place in 1988 at the University of Leuven in Belgium. Next year (1992) will see the Fifth Forum on the Person-Centred Approach to be held in the Netherlands: others have taken place in Mexico (the first in 1982), England, the USA and Brazil. These international gatherings demonstrate that Rogers' ideas are powerfully alive and that there is a large community of therapists and scholars throughout the world who are committed to the person-centred approach and to the continuation of a distinctive school of psychotherapy with its separate orientation based on Rogers' work. As Professor Germain Lietaer put it in his comments at the end of the Leuven conference:

> We are just too good to be absorbed (in a superficial way) by other orientations. Our richness should not be lost. Along with the psychoanalytic, 'systems', and behavioural approaches, I think there remains a need for a more phenomenological-experiential-existential approach. (Lietaer, 1990: 39)

The representation at the recent conference in Stirling was impressive. Nearly 260 delegates were drawn from 28 different countries and almost 100 presentations were made during the week. The range of subjects addressed showed that conference members were involved in almost every possible aspect of therapeutic activity. Papers covered themes as widely diverse as 'The pre-symbolic structure and processing of schizophrenic hallucinations', 'Documented myths in psychotherapy outcome research' and 'Person-centred therapy with children and adolescents'. It appears that the vitality of Rogers' legacy is currently assured and that those who embrace his ideas are increasingly aware of the importance of their inheritance and of the responsibility which is now theirs to preserve and develop an approach which, through its fundamental trust in the client, stands in stark contrast to the standard clinical mandate that the therapist should be in control and determine the experiences of the client in therapy.

The international strength of the orientation often seems to take even experienced practitioners by surprise. Rogers himself was highly ambivalent about institutions and associations, so little or nothing was done until the final years of his life to give shape or coherence to the growing world community of those whose professional activity was based on his ideas and example. Rogers feared that the establishment of some kind of international association or society would inevitably lead to the development of doctrinal rigidity and the imposition of accreditation or admission procedures, which he abhorred. He was not reassured by the history of client-centred associations in some European countries, where precisely the kind of exclusivity he feared had come about. The forums and conferences of the last decade have done much, despite the lack of a central organization, to establish an international identity for the approach but even as late as 1987 David Cain, editor of the *Person-Centered Review*, could write of his astonishment when a few years earlier he had become aware for the first time of the enormous influence of Rogers' work.

> While Carl Rogers' work is well known by most American psychologists and educators, many of these same professionals are little aware of the global impact of his ideas. Carl Rogers' work has reached over 25 countries. His writings have been translated into 12 languages. In 1984, while attending the Second International Forum on the Person-Centered Approach in Norwich, England, I remember feeling astonished over the enormous impact Rogers was having abroad. My impression was that his ideas were more enthusiastically received and more influential in many other countries than in the United States. Whether this is true or not is difficult, if not impossible, to say. However, it does seem safe to say that the person-centred approach is known to hundreds of thousands of persons throughout the world who employ Carl Rogers' ideas in their professional and/or personal lives. Many continue to develop, refine, and expand the theory and application of the person-centered approach. Our family of scholars and practitioners is truly an international one. (Cain, 1987a: 139)

In the same article Cain goes on to give a brief overview of the nature and range of person-centred activities occurring in many countries in which Rogers' work has had an influence. In the course of this he draws attention to developments in the Netherlands, Switzerland, Great Britain, Sweden, Spain, France, Italy, Hungary, Belgium, Germany, Ireland, Denmark, Norway, Austria, Japan, Australia, Brazil, Argentina, Chile, Uruguay, Peru,

Columbia, Venezuela, Mexico, South Africa, the United States and Canada. Looking through the names of intending participants at the recent Stirling Conference it seems that the following countries can now be added to Cain's list: Czechoslovakia, Greece, Israel, Malta, Poland, Portugal, Singapore, Yugoslavia and Russia. By any standards this is an impressive list, covering as it does not only a vast geographical terrain but a wide variety of cultures and political systems.

Orthodoxy and Heresy

Since Rogers' death in 1987 various different factions have begun to emerge amongst those who seek to embrace and develop his ideas. The death of great men seems almost invariably to lead to the emergence of different 'camps' among subsequent generations and in Rogers' case this may have been inevitable because of his refusal to be party to any 'tablets of stone' and his insistence on the primacy of values, attitudes and a shared philosophy rather than on techniques and particular therapeutic strategies. For him, it was always of critical importance that students and trainees should be free to develop their own special and unique ways of implementing the core conditions and of giving expression to their profound regard for the wisdom and the constructive capacity inherent in the human organism. He could not tolerate the thought of producing 'clones' of himself and the adjective 'Rogerian' was one he always rejected with deep distaste.

Professor Jerold Bozarth of the University of Georgia was troubled by many of the presentations made at the 1988 Leuven conference because, for him, they were at variance with the essence of the client-centred/person-centred paradigm which, he believes, differentiates Rogers' approach from other therapies. Bozarth and his colleague, Barbara Temaner Brodley from Illinois, are vocal defenders of what might be described as a 'purist' position. They support their stance through their study of Rogers' writings, tapes and films from which they conclude that throughout his professional career Rogers did not alter his fundamental views of client-centred therapy. Although Temaner Brodley's most recent research reveals shifts in Rogers' behaviour as a therapist both she and Bozarth support a functional theoretical premiss that: 'The essence of client-centred/person-centred therapy is the therapist's dedication to going with the client's direction, at the client's pace, and with the client's unique way of being' (Temaner Brodley, 1988).

For Bozarth, the implications of the essence of client-centred/person-centred therapy expressed in these terms are staggering. In his paper given at the Leuven conference he writes:

> *It is a functional premise that precludes other therapist intentions.* The therapist goes with the client – goes at the client's pace – goes with the client in his/her own ways of thinking, of experiencing, of processing. *The therapist cannot be up to other things, have other intentions without violating the essence of client-centred/person-centred therapy.* To be up to other things –whatever they might be – is a 'yes, but' reaction to the essence of the approach. (Bozarth, 1990: 63)

There are many who would agree with Bozarth and Temaner Brodley and who believe that attempts to add other therapeutic methods to client-centred therapy are a betrayal of the approach. Bozarth and Temaner Brodley maintain that their functional premiss in no way precludes therapist personality differences, unique ways of doing things and idiosyncratic modes of responding to clients. They are, however, utterly opposed to the notion that client-centred therapists have the option to introduce into their work with clients skills and strategies culled from other traditions. They are hostile to the view of Professor Reinhard Tausch of Hamburg, for example, who at the same Leuven conference talked of just such an injection of other methods as a 'client-centred necessity'. In a controversial paper he advocates, as 'desirable supplementations', relaxation techniques, non-systematic behavioural counselling, problem analysis, medical treatment and recommending books on philosophical, religious and spiritual issues. He prefaces this advocacy of a veritable psychological programme with the firm assertion:

> it is obvious from daily practical experience that we as client-centred psychotherapists help some of our clients only insufficiently. This is in agreement with our empirical results from the doctoral theses of a research project on individual therapies with approximately 200 clients, and on group-psychotherapy with 350 clients. (Tausch, 1990: 447)

Bozarth and Tausch are both 'senior members' of the international community and it is striking that they should have moved to such diametrically opposed positions. In brief, Bozarth believes that Rogers' work is of unique importance and that its essence is immediately contaminated if other methods are introduced and control is in any way removed from the client. Tausch, one of the most prolific researchers of psychotherapy outcomes in the world, believes, on the other hand, that in those cases where 'pure' client-centred therapy seems not to work the therapist should have no hesitation in offering other possible strategies to his client. The gap between the 'purist' orthodoxy and the heretical 'supplementation school' is considerable, yet adherents of both find in Rogers the inspiration and the defence for their positions. Tausch and those of like mind cite Rogers' eminently pragmatic approach and his concern with 'what works' while Bozarth and his colleagues fear that such a dilution of Rogers' commitment to the client's path will inevitably lead to the gradual disappearance of client-centred therapy as a separate and unique orientation in its own right. For the moment both camps exist in somewhat uneasy alliance although there is unresolved tension on both sides. I had always considered myself to be somewhat of a 'purist' until a member of the 'purist camp' walked out of a video demonstration of my work when he witnessed what was clearly, for him, a directive response from me to my client, even if delivered with extreme respect and tentativeness. At that moment, in his eyes, I had ceased to practise client-centred therapy. I sense that Carl Rogers would have stayed to see what happened next.

The Case of Eugene Gendlin

The Stirling conference, and the Leuven conference which preceded it, had in its title reference not only to client-centred but also to *experiential* psychotherapy. The conference organizers in both cases were clear in their intention that they wished to see at these international gatherings those practitioners for whom not only Carl Rogers but also Eugene Gendlin constituted a major influence. Gendlin, a former close associate of Rogers, conceptualized experiential psychotherapy in the 1960s and has always viewed it as theoretically consistent with and in some ways an improvement on client-centred therapy. Certainly Gendlin has the distinction of being the first client-centred therapist to develop a distinctive approach, with its own enthusiastic adherents, which is clearly derived from Rogers' work. Gendlin's major contribution lies in his understanding of the experiencing process which takes place within the client during therapy. He believes that therapeutic movement occurs when the level of experiencing is high and is accompanied by a bodily felt sense. Gendlin developed a method, which he calls 'focusing', whereby the therapist could assist the client to achieve such a level of experiencing and to use specific bodily feelings as a referent for discovering new meanings (Gendlin, 1978). Gendlin maintains that focusing is a way of enabling clients to make contact with the deepest levels of experience by paying attention to an unclear sense of 'something there'. He is understandably enthusiastic about 'focusing' and he and his associates have taught the technique to thousands of people in the past twenty years. There is no doubt that it can be powerfully effective in enabling clients to locate and clarify feelings that are on the 'edge of awareness'. For many therapists, who would claim the label experiential rather than client-centred, focusing is an activity which they would aim to encourage in their clients and it is precisely this aim that brings down upon Gendlin and his followers the wrath of the 'purists'. Barbara Temaner Brodley has been particularly critical, for she sees the experiential therapists as essentially directive in intent and therefore as having forsaken the basic principles of client-centred therapy.

> The theory as written and illustrated by Gendlin makes it clear that the therapist's primary and active responsibility – that is, what the therapist should do in working with his client – is to *direct* the client toward the focused experiencing process and help the client to maintain a 'high experiencing level'. (Temaner Brodley, 1990: 89)

Critics of experiential therapy see it as essentially lacking in trust that the client will find his or her own way forward without the active and directive intervention of the therapist in relation to the experiencing process. It is no longer the primary concern of the therapist to provide the therapeutic attitudes but rather to ensure that the client experiences in the manner and at the level for therapy to occur.

In answer to questions at the Leuven conference Gendlin categorically refuted the suggestion that experiential therapy is a false development from Rogers' work. In reply to Barbara Temaner Brodley's challenge to explore the difference between client-centred and experiential psychotherapy he said:

> I would take client-centred therapy to be the larger thing. . . . What I call focusing is paying attention inwardly to that unclear sense of something there. Now surely therapy and personal development are much bigger things than that. Focusing is a very deliberate way to touch something inside. I have seen that help the bigger process. The bigger process comes from behind you and takes you and expands you, and you do not know what is going to happen. Whereas focusing is this very deliberate thing where an 'I' is attending to an 'it'. I think it is very valuable. But surely it is not therapy. Therapy is a relationship, therapy is a process of development. These focusing steps I described come in client centred therapy. That is where I learnt them from, that is where I saw them and if you observe your clients, you will see that they are silent before these steps typically come. (Gendlin, 1990: 222)

Doubtless the debate will continue, but it was noticeable at the Stirling conference that some of the heat seemed to have gone out of the conflict. The experiential therapists were present in greater numbers and seemed full of energy and self-confidence. The 'purists' seemed to adopt a parental rather than a judgemental role as if they had come to accept that the Gendlin supporters, were, after all, members of the same family. It seemed to be the turn of the 'supplementation school' to keep a low profile in plenary sessions but papers with such titles as 'Personal construct theory for client-centred therapy' and 'Integration of methods or integration of therapeutic treatment' showed that they had by no means renounced their heretical tendencies.

Expressive Therapies

A new presence on the scene at the Stirling conference was a small group of therapists who are working with the expressive arts while remaining true to the person-centred philosophy. Much of this work is inspired by the pioneering training of Carl Rogers' daughter, Natalie, who directs the Person-centered Expressive Therapy Institute in Santa Rosa, California. Movement, art, music, pottery, dream exploration and writing all feature in this approach and clients who have grave difficulty in expressing themselves verbally find new possibilities for self-expression through essentially non-verbal channels. The approach attracts the inevitable criticism that it fosters too directive an attitude in the therapist but the creation of the facilitative conditions is essential to its success and there is no sense in which clients are coerced into forms of expression which they have not willingly embraced. Rogers is sometimes criticized for being altogether too verbal in his approach and for pandering to the articulate middle class. It is somehow appropriate that his daughter should be chiefly instrumental in the training of person-centred therapists for whom verbalization is the least preferred mode of expression.

Indirect Influence

While Rogers' life and work have led to the creation of an established school of psychotherapy with its own internal divisions and differences, it is difficult to assess his *indirect* influence on psychotherapy and helping relationships in general. At various points in this book I have alluded to his apparent importance even for those who disagree with his views and I have suggested that his contribution to the spread of 'lay therapy' and to the humanizing of relationships in many different professional fields has been immense. Certainly Rogers himself believed this to be the case. On many occasions, both in private and in his published articles and books, he expressed awe and amazement at the influence his work had had in various professional spheres and in many different countries. In part, the influence is attributable to his prolific writing: Rogers wrote sixteen books and more than 200 professional articles and research studies, which were read and continue to be read by many thousands of people. He was a communicator of rare ability and his books in particular have a quality about them which tends to make the reader come away from them feeling good.

This capacity to validate others through the written word is a natural outcome of Rogers' deep respect for the uniqueness of persons and of his desire to facilitate their development. There are some, however, who believe that this very capacity has led to the unfortunate situation where Rogers can appear to be giving his blessing to almost any form of therapy on the score that every practitioner must find his own style and way of operating. It is as if Rogers, through his deep acceptance and empathic understanding, has given licence to therapists of widely differing orientations to claim allegiance to him – and even to call themselves client-centred or person-centred – although they have, in fact, departed completely from the basic philosophy and principles of the approach he advocates. For members of the 'purist' camp this is intolerable and that is why they are so uneasy about their 'supplementation' colleagues; they see in some of their activities the thin end of a wedge which could rapidly lead to practices totally at variance with client-centred principles. C.H. Patterson, in a heartfelt article in the special issue of the *Person-Centered Review* to celebrate the fiftieth anniversary of the person-centred approach, sums the matter up with characteristic bluntness:

> Are there no limits to what can be called client-centered? Is anything that is done by a therapist claiming to be client-centered actually client-centered? Did Rogers, in his modesty and openness to new ideas, issue a licence for client-centered therapists to do whatever they feel like doing and still claim to be client-centered? (Patterson, 1990: 427)

The issue of the indirect influence of Rogers is rendered the more complex by this confusion for it seems that many therapists *claim* to be influenced by Rogers who have, in fact, failed completely to understand the essential core of his work. It is difficult to know how to identify let alone how to evaluate such an influence, which often seems to be a *misunderstood* influence. I find myself sympathizing greatly with John K. Wood, for years one of Rogers' closest associates, who despairingly responded to the question: 'What is most essential to the continued development of the theory and application of the person-centred approach?' in these terms:

> The question is meaningless. There is no *the* person-centered approach.

To client-centered therapists trained at the University of Chicago it is a method of one-to-one psychotherapy backed by theory and research – although the research has become equivocal. To academics it is the foundation for counselor training programs though they differ as to whether its value is realized by applying behavioral techniques or by adopting a special attitude. . . .

If we speak of client-centered therapy . . . I don't know any behavior therapist, psychoanalyst, or humanistic psychotherapist who doesn't readily admit to being influenced by its principles. Still, no one I can think of, with the exception of Goff Barrett-Lennard and Nat Raskin [two early students of Rogers], has said to me that they are client-centered therapists. Most people repeat vacuously the cliché: 'I believe that Rogers' conditions are necessary, but not sufficient'. Some of Rogers' closest colleagues use hypnosis, guided fantasies, paradoxical statements, dream analysis, exercises, give home-work assignments and generally follow the latest fads to supply their missing sufficiency. (Wood, 1986: 350–1)

We are left, then, with the overwhelming impression that Rogers' indirect influence on the whole field of counselling and psychotherapy has been immense, and yet at the same time it seems impossibly difficult to evaluate how the influence has been experienced and received. To quote John Wood again: 'In short, it [the person-centered approach] is everything and nothing.' David Cain, in his editorial to the 50th anniversary edition of the *Person-Centered Review* struggles with the same issue and is bold enough to attempt a more precise account of Rogers' contribution. His list of major ways in which Rogers and his colleagues influenced the whole field of counselling and psychotherapy includes:

1. Emphasizing the importance of the therapeutic relationship as a healing agent in therapy.
2. Articulating a view of the person as inherently resourceful and self-actualizing.
3. Developing the art of listening and understanding and demonstrating its therapeutic effect on the client.
4. Introducing the term, *client* as opposed to *patient*, to convey greater respect, dignity and a quality of the person seeking help.
5. Initiating the sound recordings of therapeutic interviews for learning purposes and informal research.
6. Initiating scientific research on the process and outcome of psychotherapy.
7. Paving the way for psychologists and other non-medical professionals to engage in the practice of psychotherapy.

Later in his article, Cain observes:

To a large degree Rogers' impact has been indirect. Consequently, the magnitude of his impact is difficult to assess. If I were to venture a guess about how Rogers' contributions might be assessed on their 100th anniversary (2040), I would predict that the most enduring and meaningful contributions for which he will be remembered are the therapeutic impact of *listening* and the quality of the *therapist–client relationship*. Although many practitioners do not find Rogers' style of listening and responding congenial, almost all recognize the importance of empathy and the desirability of a sound working relationship with the client. (Cain, 1990: 357–8)

I find myself in broad agreement with Cain and would like to believe that his overall judgement is soundly based. I realize, however, that 'recognizing the importance of empathy' is not the same as being able to offer empathy and I am reminded of Rogers' own despair at the lack of training which many therapists still have in developing their empathic capacities. This, in turn, makes me question whether Rogers' example has really brought about a revolution in the art of listening. Eugene Gendlin is certainly doubtful about this and goes so far as to attach blame to client-centred practitioners for their failure to communicate the power of listening to colleagues from other orientations. At the Leuven conference he addressed this issue with some passion:

It is unbelievable that after all these years, we have totally failed to communicate client-centered listening in such a way that *other* practitioners could have it. How can they go so long without it? How can they be so stupid? But then, I realize, that is largely our fault. We have told them that if one does client-centered listening, then one does nothing else, so, of course they cannot have it because they are already doing something else and they know that that is helpful. They are not going to give that up. They cannot 'unknow' what they know. (Gendlin, 1990: 207)

Doubtless many from the 'purist' camp would question the motivation behind Gendlin's listening, yet his comment throws a shadow over the perhaps too readily accepted assumption that Rogers has brought about a revolution in therapists' ability to listen and to empathize. It may be that, thanks to Rogers and his writings, there is now a much greater *awareness* of the importance of listening and of empathy in the therapeutic relationship, but awareness of itself does not necessarily mean that there is any great increase in the *ability* of most therapists to listen and to empathize.

Training

In his rather scathing comments about the incoherence of the person-centred approach Wood suggests that Rogers' ideas form the basis of many counsellor training programmes, although he goes on to indicate the lack of real understanding which often lies behind this apparently positive state of affairs. It appears that Rogers' functional philosophy is often reduced to a clutch of techniques passed on to trainees in the form of interpersonal skills, which they learn to deploy often through structured exercises. Their level of competence is sometimes measured through the use of 'rating scales', especially in the case of empathy where discrete counsellor responses are assessed for their level of empathic accuracy. This attempt to reduce the offering of a core condition to a series of structured steps at which trainees can work systematically owes much to the work of Robert Carkhuff (1969) and Gerard Egan (1975). Many have benefited from this particular kind of introduction to 'counselling skills', but it seems highly questionable whether such training procedures can be viewed as a legitimate development of Rogers' work. They seem rather to be an adaptation of certain research methods which, as we have seen, were of somewhat questionable value even in that context. Rogers himself discovered very early on in his career that the learning of acceptant and empathic responses to clients did not in itself lead to therapeutic effectiveness. Acceptant and empathic *behaviours*, it seemed, were powerless to effect change if they did not spring from deeply held and integrated *convictions* about the nature of human beings and of the therapeutic process.

Doubts about the extent of Rogers' influence on therapy training programmes are to some extent intensified by the fact that few well-established programmes exist worldwide for the specific training of client-centred or person-centred therapists. Rogers saw this as one outcome of the under-representation of person-centred practitioners in the universities. Writing in 1986, principally about research, he said:

> We are underrepresented partly because we constitute a threat to the academically minded. We espouse the importance of experiential as well as cognitive learning. Such learning involves the risk of being changed by the experience, and this can be frightening to one whose world is intellectually structured. Perhaps partly due to this aspect, there are few faculty members who have been trained in, or even exposed to, a person-centred approach. (Rogers, 1986a: 257–8)

At the recent Stirling conference an informal meeting of trainers revealed that the overall situation is gradually improving. In the United States and elsewhere there are some institutionally based programmes, and a number of rigorous courses are developing in the private sector sponsored both by independent training institutes and by person-centred associations and societies. Britain is well represented in this respect with courses run by Person-Centred Therapy (Britain) and the Person Centred Approach Institute

International. The PCT course is recognized by the British Association for Counselling and the PCAII course has good links with other programmes offered by the Institute in Europe. In the public sector a Diploma in Counselling is offered at the Wigan College of Technology which is strongly influenced by Rogers' ideas and practice. This, too, is one of the few courses currently recognized by the British Association for Counselling. At the international level the Center for the Studies of the Person in La Jolla is about to launch a training programme staffed by leading practitioners from many parts of the world. The directors of this course are Maria Bowen and Suzanne Spector, both long-standing members of the Center and close colleagues of Rogers. Britain is represented on the staff by Dave Mearns of PCT (Britain) and Jordanhill College, Glasgow. Mearns has ambitious plans for both full- and part-time courses at Jordanhill which will add greatly to the opportunities for person-centred training within the British statutory sector. It is perhaps appropriate that Jordanhill is to become a centre for person-centred training for the College is still primarily concerned with the education of teachers. The appropriateness lies in the fact that Rogers' influence in Britain was first experienced in a major way through the courses set up in the mid-1960s to train school counsellors in this country. It was in education institutes at the Universities of Keele and Reading that American Fulbright Fellows, trained in the client-centred tradition, first introduced British teachers to Rogers' ideas. The graduates from these courses – and also subsequently from the course for counsellors in higher education at the University of Aston – have made a profound impact on the development of counselling in Britain not only in educational settings but more generally. Rogers once expressed pleasure that the infiltration of his ideas and practice into Britain seemed to owe more to the efforts of pioneering figures from the world of education than to the psychological or medical establishment.

Research

Despite differences in clinical practice there is one thing on which all are agreed. This was summed up by Rogers in 1986 when he stated categorically: 'What we need most is solid research.' This theme was a leitmotif throughout Rogers' life and we have seen how the scientist in him remained alert until the end. Whether it was in the early pioneering days, when he was deeply committed to the methodology of logical positivism, or in the later years when he was excited by new developments in the philosophy of science which pointed to new phenomenologically based methods, Rogers never doubted for a moment that psychotherapy needed research backing if it was to develop its effectiveness. In this his influence has been all-pervasive. That is not to say that researchers have now succeeded in discovering perfect investigative methods for exploring the complex processes of psychotherapy, but it does mean that many therapists are now concerned that their work should be subjected to research scrutiny. Research findings are now more likely than ever before to affect training procedures and clinical practice across many different therapeutic orientations. In some ways it is ironical and somewhat amusing that Rogers, who is often criticized for being naive and too tender-hearted, should have been chiefly instrumental in bringing about such apparently hard-headed developments.

Beyond the Consulting Room

A further major difficulty in assessing Rogers' overall influence on counselling and psychotherapy is the fact that, unlike most other professional therapists, he was not content to remain in his consulting room. There are those who profoundly regret this and would much have preferred him to have stayed at the University of Chicago and to have continued in patient clinical practice and research until retirement, to the undoubted benefit of subsequent generations of therapists throughout the world. Instead he chose to move out into the untidy confusion of encounter groups, cross-cultural communication, peace work and what cynics regarded as a mission to convert the world to the person-centred approach. Some have never forgiven him for this apparent grandiosity of intent, and very recently one of his former students and associates, Dr Bill Coulson, hit the headlines by launching a full-scale attack on what he considers the grave error Rogers made of generalizing from insights formulated in the counselling room to conclusions about how life should be lived in families, schools and society at large. Coulson currently appears on American radio and television and testifies before legislative committees on education, drug abuse and juvenile delinquency. He believes that both he and Rogers owe the nation's parents an apology for having so grievously misled them into thinking that their children should be offered the core conditions and encouraged to make up their own minds about the direction of their lives. So extreme has Coulson become in his denigration of the ideas of his former mentor, colleague and friend that he recently implied that Rogers repudiated his philosophy late in life and acknowledged that he was in error. Howard Kirschen-baum, Rogers' biographer, has felt obliged to answer Coulson and to dismiss as totally without foundation the suggestion that Rogers in any way repudiated his beliefs (Kirschenbaum, 1991). What is particularly interesting about this whole bizarre sequence of events is Coulson's apparent conviction that Rogers' ideas have had and are continuing to have such a powerful effect on people's lives. The passion and intensity of Coulson's campaign can only be explained by his belief that Rogers' ideas are transforming society and that the transformation is pernicious.

It is perhaps significant that Bill Coulson is a committed Roman Catholic and it appears that his current zeal is fired by the realization that for him Rogers' ideas and beliefs had become a modern-day religious system. Interestingly, Coulson does not refute the basic tenets of client-centred therapy, which he still believes to be correct: his quarrel is with the application of discoveries made about psychotherapy to other areas of human life – notably education and the family unit. This particular crusade will doubtless run its course and soon be forgotten but the issues at the heart of the affair are, I believe, both fascinating and important.

As someone who has frequently facilitated person-centred encounter groups in many parts of the world and often been a member of cross-cultural communities, I am well aware of the transforming effect such groups can have on many participants. There is a sense in which these experiences can lead to a greatly heightened sense of awareness and a much enhanced feeling both of self-worth and of interconnectedness with others. The encounter group can provide an avenue into a level of experiencing which can appropriately be described as spiritual, mystical, transcendental (Thorne, 1988: 201). Such experiences are naturally short lived, but they touch people at the deepest level and often leave them both exhilarated and disturbed. For those who have no previous experience of such intensity and no religious or spiritual framework into which they can 'fit' what has happened to them, the underpinning philosophy of Rogers' work becomes their credo. What they have experienced is of a spiritual order so it is understandable that they should elevate Rogers' ideas and the person-centred 'movement' to the same level. Rogers' ideas then become all-embracing and affect every aspect of their lives – and that, for Bill Coulson, is where the trouble begins.

Coulson's current perturbation was foreshadowed by Paul Vitz in his book *Psychology as Religion* which appeared in 1977 and to which reference was made in the previous chapter. Vitz argues persuasively that the most direct source for what he describes as contemporary 'humanistic selfism' is Ludwig Feuerbach's *The Essence of Christianity* which first appeared in 1841. The book was an influential attack on Christianity in so far as Feuerbach postulated that God is merely the projected essence of man and that the highest law of ethics is that man's selfless love for humanity constitutes salvation. Feuerbach argued that what was formerly viewed and worshipped as God is now recognized as something human. Man becomes man's God. Feuerbach, in Vitz's estimation, directly or indirectly affected the thinking of Marx, Nietzsche, Huxley, John Stuart Mill and – most significantly – Freud and Dewey. Rogers fits neatly at the end of this line of descent as the disciple of Dewey through the mediation of William Heard Kilpatrick.

Vitz is not content with citing Rogers' essentially anti-Christian precursors. He discovers that in the United States there were popular Protestant ministers during the period from 1920 to the mid-1950s who embraced such concepts as 'self-realization', 'becoming a real person' and the primacy of becoming over being without abandoning the Christian church. In Vitz's eyes their Christianity was a strangely emasculated and superficial version of the true faith yet it is clear that their message had great appeal for many Americans who did not wish to jettison a religious view of reality. Vitz quotes in particular the work of Harry Emerson Fosdick and Norman Vincent Peale and draws somewhat ironical attention to the fact that Fosdick's *On Being a Real Person* (1943) preceded Rogers' *On Becoming a Person* by almost twenty years. Both Fosdick and Peale were deeply involved in pastoral counselling and drew extensively on contemporary psychological insights. Vitz notes that for Fosdick integration and self-realization replaced the theological concept of salvation. In Vitz's view the period of Fosdick and Peale was one of transition, which responded to the needs of a population disenchanted with basic Christian theology and ignorant of real spirituality but still unwilling to relinquish a religious framework. The post-World War II generation, however, was ready for a humanistic selfism which had finally lost the trappings of the diluted Christianity of their parents' generation. The time was ripe for humanistic psychology to come into its own and Carl Rogers was to become the acknowledged leader not only of a psychological 'third force' to challenge the ascendancy of analysis and behaviourism but also, in Vitz's eyes, of an applied philosophy which amounted to a new secular religion (Vitz, 1977: 66–82).

Vitz and other writers find further historical precedents for Rogers' later work with encounter groups and large communities in the Christian pietism and Jewish Hasidism of the eighteenth and nineteenth centuries. More recently, in a paper presented at the Stirling conference, Louise Yeoman of St Andrew's University,

Scotland also discovers unlikely parallels with person-centred therapy in the experience of seventeenth-century Calvinists (Yeoman, 1991). Fascinating as these similarities are their chief relevance in attempting to assess Rogers' overall influence lies in the fact that experiences of personal growth and interpersonal intimacy akin to those recorded by participants in person-centred contexts have in the past commonly been associated with a religious and spiritual understanding of reality. It is scarcely surprising that at the present time the process seems to be operating in the reverse direction: the 'secular' experience of person-centred groups in particular seems for some people to open up a channel into spiritual terrain which has previously remained unexplored and whose very existence has been denied.

It is my own conviction that Rogers' early experiences, however perverse the theology underpinning them, ensured that his understanding of subjective phenomena and of interpersonal relationships could not in the end fail to embrace what, in his own words, he described as the transcendent, the indescribable, the spiritual. For Coulson and for Vitz such language is presumably a sinister indication of the grandiosity of a psychotherapeutic approach which aspires to become a philosophy of life or, even worse, a substitute religion. Both condemn Rogers as hostile to true religion and particularly to Christianity and see his ideas as destructive of family life and detrimental to the creation of a responsible society. Vitz, indeed, places Rogers at the end of a line of thinkers who have consistently undermined Christianity since the nineteenth century. My own perception is radically different. Paradoxically, the vehemence of the attack on Rogers by such Christian apologists as Vitz and Coulson serves to reinforce my conviction that Rogers' deep ambivalence towards institutional religion is an inevitable outcome not only of his own negative experience of a constraining theology but also of his openness to experience and thus to spiritual reality. The evidence, I believe, is overwhelming that Rogers in his deep respect for human beings and in his trust of the actualizing tendency has enabled many to discover that at the deepest centre of the person and infusing the organismic self is the human spirit which is open to the transcendent. This discovery, which is the very essence of spirituality, often results in a move towards a belief in God and in the divine quality inherent in men and women which would previously have been inconceivable for those who thus find themselves unexpectedly launched on a spiritual journey. Fifty years from now it is likely that Rogers will be remembered not so much as the founder of a new school of psychotherapy but as a psychologist whose work made it possible for men and women to apprehend spiritual reality at a time when conventional religion had lost its power to capture the minds and imaginations of the vast majority. The spiritual thread in Rogers' work that remained covert and even denied for most of his professional life eventually emerges not as a mysterious dimension but as the outcome of faith in the actualizing tendency and in the power of the core conditions to bring about transformation. When Rogers spoke in 1986 of inner spirit touching inner spirit and of a therapeutic relationship transcending itself and becoming 'part of something larger' he was not deserting the 'third force' of humanistic psychology and throwing in his lot with the 'fourth force' of the transpersonal psychologists. Rogers did not set out in any conscious and deliberate way to give his 'presence' to clients and thus to sweep them up into a new spiritual reality. This fourth quality, however it is defined, was simply the outcome of his trust in the client's actualizing tendency and his commitment to the offering of the core conditions. And yet, as he discovered, and with him countless others whether therapists or clients, facilitators or members of encounter groups, the effect is totally transforming for it enables transcendence to occur so that a new perspective can be achieved. As I have written elsewhere:

> Always there is a sense of well-being, of it being good to be alive and this in spite of the fact that problems or difficulties which confront the client remain apparently unchanged and as intractable as ever. Life is good and life is impossible, long live life. (Thorne, 1985: 10)

Thoroughgoing phenomenologist that he was, Rogers never attempted to impose his version of reality on anyone else, and the same remains true when we speak of a spiritual or transcendent reality. In a remarkable article written in 1978, 'Do we need "a" reality?', Rogers concluded:

> I, and many others, have come to a new realization. It is this: The only reality I can possibly know is the world as *I* perceive and experience it at this moment. The only reality you can possibly know is the world as *you* perceive and experience it at this moment. And the only certainty is that those perceived realities are different. There are as many 'real worlds' as there are people! This creates a most burdensome dilemma, one never before experienced in history. (Rogers, 1978: 7)

It is nonetheless this 'burdensome dilemma' which Rogers' work enables us to shoulder and through it to discover freedom in transcendence. The spiritual world to which the person-centred approach often gives access is not caught up in dogmatic formulations or ethical certainties for it, too, has as many facets as there are people who experience it.

Rogers dreamt of a world where society was based on the hypothesis of multiple realities and believed that such a society would not be characterized by selfishness and anarchy. He had a vision of a community of persons no longer motivated by a blind commitment to a cause or creed or view of reality, but by a common commitment to each other as separate persons with their own separate realities. As he put it: 'The natural human tendency to care for another would no longer be "I care for you because you are the same as I" but, instead, "I prize and treasure you because you are different from me"' (Rogers, 1978: 9).

The most far-reaching of Rogers' many contributions may well turn out to be this assurance that in order to affirm our natures we do not have to put on the straitjacket of a common creed or shared dogma but can celebrate the mysterious paradox of our uniqueness and our membership one of another.

A Liberating Polytheism

In a highly original paper delivered at the Stirling conference, the Australian therapist and scholar, Bernie Neville, maintained that most therapies are 'monotheistic' in that they acknowledge one truth, one value system and one version of reality. 'Client-centred therapy is not like this,' says Neville, 'although we sometimes try to make it so by defining too single-mindedly what we take to be the truth. Neither is it mindlessly eclectic or shapelessly flexible. It has a distinctive truth and a distinctive form but both its truth and its form are comfortable with paradox' (Neville, 1991: 16). Such a therapy, Neville believes, is in keeping with the shift in consciousness which characterizes the so-called 'postmodern condition' where the myth of an absolute reality that can be made apparent to the human intellect is fast fading and is being replaced, in science as well as in philosophy, by a much more relativistic and ambiguous approach to reality. Situating Rogers in this context suggests again that his influence may only just have begun. Not only may it turn out that he affords access to spiritual and transcendent experience for thoroughly secularized men and women but it may also be that his work has within it the means for holding paradoxes in tension and for containing logical contradictions without splitting apart. Bernie Neville uses the language of archetypal psychology to present the person-centred approach as essentially polytheistic rather than monotheistic. As someone who continues to find nourishment and challenge in the Christian faith and for whom Carl Rogers has been a major influence in this continuing allegiance, I take delight in concluding this book by introducing the pantheon of gods whom Neville discovers to be in animated discourse in the life and work of Carl Rogers. If he is right then assuredly the influence of this 'quiet revolutionary' has scarcely begun. I know Dr Neville will forgive me for plundering his work in order to create this final 'group encounter'.

Athena: Person-centred therapy is beyond doubt an Athena-therapy. Its key assumption, after all, is the existence of the client's practical wisdom and his or her innate ability (however much repressed) to decide what is best. In practice, too, everything hinges on the genuine sharing of power and I believe intensely in that and in the co-operative exploration of a problem.

Hephaestos: Person-centred therapy is focused and dedicated work. I lay rightful claim to it because it takes the everyday elements of human relating and then crafts them in such a way that they become beautiful and powerful.

Prometheus: I have much sympathy with Robert Carkhuff and believe that his view of client-centred therapy is not so wide of the mark. After all, providing the core conditions demands the skills of the highly effective kind of people I admire. They are engaged in freeing their clients and students so that they can use their own personal power and become effective and resourceful people in their turn. I'm not so sure that client-centred therapy is a way of life but it is certainly an immensely powerful clutch of skills for providing the sort of people I like and respect.

Hestia: Person-centred therapy is essentially concerned with the inner work which is my chosen domain. It encourages us to turn away from frantic or desperate activity so that we can find the still point within where thinking and feeling can be integrated and clarity can emerge.

Eros: Person-centred therapy is essentially my therapy for the core of its theory and method is understanding and the practice of genuine loving.

Aphrodite: Most people worship me under the aspect of sexual attractiveness but I am also, of course, the god of spiritual beauty. However you regard me, though, I am clearly the driving force behind much of what happens in person-centred therapy. I believe that therapy often works by way of a kind of seduction so that the therapist's personality or the attractiveness of a therapist's view of life makes a powerful contribution to the client's healing. Person-centred therapists do not operate within the fantasy that the liking of client for therapist or therapist for client is irrelevant. Because I encourage a confidence in the essential beauty of human-beings my presence is central to the therapeutic process and person-centred therapists can acknowledge this with delight and without embarrassment.

Dionysos: Person-centred therapy clearly belongs to me for its essential theoretical notion is the existence of the actualizing tendency, the drive towards the emergence of the true, vital, spontaneous self from the sterility of introjected values and incongruent behaviour.

Ares: I must certainly have a major place for Rogers' work is essentially about confrontation, about facing oneself and one's world as they are without pretence. There is nothing cosy or unchallenging about this approach. Therapist and client need me as they wrestle with demons and dragons in the struggle for self-discovery.

Demeter: Person-centred therapy is essentially my domain for as the Great Mother I know that its effectiveness comes through the therapist's ability to offer support and nourishment. Person-centred therapy provides the mother's warm embrace to the client whose immediate need is to be childlike and dependent. Later, when the time comes, I can assist that child to grow towards maturity, but only when the time is ripe.

Artemis: I am the essential midwife in client-centred therapy who sits beside the client in whom new life is struggling to be born. I affirm what is natural and what is genuine and I uphold them against a pathological patriarchy which desires their exploitation and destruction.

Apollo: I am the preserver of the early Carl Rogers who values scientific research and sees it as vital for understanding the therapeutic process. I assist the therapist as he seeks to help the client to clarify, to symbolize, to find meaning. Client-centred therapy belongs to me for it recognizes that we all need to construct a meaning for our lives and that our behaviour needs to be consistent with that meaning.

Hera: I am the Queen of the gods and I attend to the stability of the family and of social structure. I preserve Rogers from the accusation of encouraging narcissism and cultural anarchy. I stood by him in his own development and I am the influence which tells him that the actualizing tendency takes us towards greater interdependence with others and that clients as they progress in therapy become more accepting of others, more socially aware and concerned. I am there always in the therapist's loyalty and commitment to her clients. I uphold the dignity of every single person and I never give up on anyone.

Zeus: I fear I am Carl Rogers' blind spot for he seems to see authority as essentially abusive. When he talked with Buber he seemed unable to acknowledge what to Buber was obvious – that therapist and client were not equal. I wish Rogers was not so keen to deny any interest in power although I don't want him to be turned into a Wise Old Man and his writings into sacred texts. But I take courage from the fact that he wanted to be *influential* because I believe he is and will be more so as the years go by – that is if those who embrace his ideas do not allow *their* power and authority to get lost in the 'shadow'.

Hermes: I am the really important god in the Carl Rogers pantheon and it is right I should have the last word. I am a complex personality and I am full of paradoxes but when the other gods quarrel – as they do continually – I remain on friendly terms with them all. I untie knots and I am the companion and protector of travellers and sense intuitively their thoughts and feelings. I have no message of my own but I listen and reflect and carry information. I acknowledge all the gods and support their worship. Even if I am at times more than a little seductive, I never lose my sense of the sacred. (Adapted from Neville, 1991: 16–19)

A Select Bibliography of the Works of Carl Rogers

In the list that follows those works which are marked with an asterisk are regarded as key texts.

Books

Counseling and Psychotherapy: Newer Concepts in Practice (1942). Boston: Houghton Mifflin.

*Client-Centered Therapy: Its Current Practice, Implications and Theory (1951). Boston: Houghton Mifflin. (Other editions include: London, Constable, 1965).

With R. Dymond (eds) *Psychotherapy and Personality Change* (1954). Chicago: University of Chicago Press.

*On Becoming a Person (1961). Boston: Houghton Mifflin. (Other editions include: London, Constable, 1974).

Freedom to Learn: a View of What Education Might Become (1969). Columbus, OH: Charles E. Merrill.

*Carl Rogers on Personal Power: Inner Strength and its Revolutionary Impact (1977). New York: Delacorte Press. (Other editions include: London, Constable, 1978).

*A Way of Being (1980). Boston: Houghton Mifflin.

Freedom to Learn in the '80s (1983). Colombus, OH: Charles Merrill.

Two recent edited 'anthologies' have appeared which provide an excellent overview of Rogers' work as well as including hitherto unavailable material:

Kirschenbaum, H. and Henderson, V.L. (eds) (1990). *The Carl Rogers Reader*. London: Constable.

Kirschenbaum, H. and Henderson, V.L. (eds) (1990). *Carl Rogers: Dialogues*. London: Constable.

Articles

'A note on the "nature of man"' (1957). *Journal of Counseling Psychology*, 4(3): 199-203.

*'The necessary and sufficient conditions of therapeutic personality change' (1957). *Journal of Counseling Psychology*, 21(2): 95-103.

*'A theory of therapy, personality and interpersonal relationships, as developed in the client-centered framework' (1959). In S. Koch (ed.), *Psychology: a Study of*

Science, Vol. III. Formulations of the Person and the Social Context. New York: McGraw-Hill.

'The characteristics of a helping relationship' (1958). *Personnel and Guidance Journal*, 37: 6–16.

'Toward a modern approach to values: the valuing process in the mature person' (1964). *Journal of Abnormal and Social Psychology*, 68(2): 160–7.

'The formative tendency' (1978). *Journal of Humanistic Psychology*, 18(1): 23–6.

*'Do we need a reality?' (1978). *Dawnpoint*, 1(2): 6–9.

'Toward a more human science of the person' (1985). *Journal of Humanistic Psychology*, 25(4): 7–24.

*'A client-centered/person-centered approach to therapy' (1986). In I. Kutash and A. Wolf (eds), *Psychotherapist's Casebook*. San Francisco: Jossey-Bass. pp. 197–208.

*With R. Sanford 'Client-centered psychotherapy' (1989). In H.I. Kaplan and B.J. Sadock (eds), *Comprehensive Textbook of Psychiatry, V*. Baltimore: Williams & Wilkins. pp. 1482–501.

References

Allchin, A.M. (1988) *Participation in God*. London: Darton, Longman & Todd.

Aspy, D. and Roebuck, F.N. (1983) 'Researching person-centered issues in education', in C.R. Rogers (ed.), *Freedom to Learn in the '80s*. Columbus, OH: Charles Merrill.

Barrineau, P. (1990) 'Chicago revisited: an interview with Elizabeth Sheerer', *Person-Centered Review*, 5(4): 416–24.

Bozarth, J. (1990) 'The essence of client-centered therapy', in G. Lietaer, J. Rombauts and R. Van Balen (eds), *Client-Centered and Experiential Psychotherapy in the Nineties*. Leuven: Leuven University Press. pp. 59–64.

Buber, M. (1937) *I and Thou* (Trans. W. Kaufmann, 1970). New York: Charles Scribner's Sons.

Burton, A. (1972) *Twelve Therapists*. San Francisco: Jossey-Bass.

Cain, D. (1987a) 'Our international family', *Person-Centered Review*, 2(2): 139–49.

Cain, D. (1987b) 'Carl Rogers's life in review', *Person-Centered Review*, 2(4): 476–506.

Cain, D. (1990) 'Celebration, reflection and renewal', *Person-Centered Review*, 5(4): 357–63.

Carkhuff, R.R. (1969) *Helping and Human Relations*. New York: Holt, Rinehart & Winston.

Egan, G. (1975) *The Skilled Helper*. Monterey, CA: Brooks/Cole.

Fosdick, H.E. (1943) *On Being a Real Person*. New York: Harper.

Freud, S. (1962) *Civilization and its Discontents*. New York: W.W. Norton.

Gendlin, E.T. (1978) *Focusing*. New York: Everest House.

Gendlin, E.T. (1990) 'The small steps of the therapy process: how they come and how to help them come', in G. Lietaer, J. Rombauts and R. Van Balen (eds), *Client-Centered and Experiential Psychotherapy in the Nineties*. Leuven: Leuven University Press. pp. 205–24.

Kirschenbaum, H. (1979) *On Becoming Carl Rogers*. New York: Delacorte Press.

Kirschenbaum, H. (1991) 'Denigrating Carl Rogers: William Coulson's last crusade', *Journal of Counseling and Development*, 69: 411–13.

Kirschenbaum, H. and Henderson, V.L. (eds) (1990a) *The Carl Rogers Reader*. London: Constable.

Kirschenbaum, H. and Henderson, V.L. (eds) (1990b) *Carl Rogers: Dialogues*. London: Constable.

Levant, R.F. and Shlien, J.M. (eds) (1984) *Client-Centered Therapy and the Person-Centered Approach*. New York: Praeger.

Liebermann, E.J. (1985) *Acts of Will: The Life and Work of Otto Rank*. New York: Free Press.

Lietaer, G. (1990) 'The client-centered approach after the Wisconsin project: a personal view on its evolution', in G. Lietaer, J. Rombauts and R. Van Balen (eds) *Client-Centered and Experiential Psychotherapy in the Nineties*. Leuven: Leuven University Press. pp. 19–45.

Masson, J. (1984) *The Assault on Truth: Freud's Suppression of the Seduction Theory*. New York: Farrar, Straus and Giroux.

Masson, J. (1989) *Against Therapy*. London: Collins.

May, R. (1982) 'The problem of evil: an open letter to Carl Rogers', *Journal of Humanistic Psychology*, 22(3): 10–21.

Mearns, D. and McLeod, J. (1984) 'A person-centered approach to research', in R.F. Levant and J.M. Shlien (eds), *Client-Centered Therapy and the Person-Centered Approach*. New York: Praeger. pp. 370–89.

Neville, B. (1991) 'Rogers, Jung and the postmodern condition'. Unpublished presentation at the Second International Conference on Client-Centred and Experiential Psychotherapy, University of Stirling, Scotland.

Nye, R.D. (1986) *Three Psychologies*, 3rd edn. Monterey, CA: Brooks/Cole.

Patterson, C.H. (1990) 'On being client-centered', *Person-Centered Review*, 5(4): 425–32.

Rank, O. (1966) 'Yale lecture', *Journal of the Otto Rank Association*, 1:12–25.

Reason, P. and Rowan, J. (eds) (1981) *Human Inquiry: a Sourcebook of New Paradigm Research*. New York: John Wiley.

Rogers, C.R. (1939) *The Clinical Treatment of the Problem Child*. Boston: Houghton Mifflin.

Rogers, C.R. (1942) *Counseling and Psychotherapy: Newer Concepts in Practice*. Boston: Houghton Mifflin.

Rogers, C.R. (1951) *Client-Centered Therapy*. Boston: Houghton Mifflin.

Rogers, C.R. (1956) 'Reinhold Niebuhr's "The Self and the Dramas of History"' *Chicago Theological Seminary Register*, 46: 13–14.

Rogers, C.R. (1957a) 'The necessary and sufficient conditions of therapeutic personality change', *Journal of Counseling Psychology*, 21(2): 95–103.

Rogers, C.R. (1957b) 'A note on the "nature of man"', *Journal of Counseling Psychology*, 4(3): 199–203.

Rogers, C.R. (1958) 'Concluding comment of discussion of R. Niebuhr's The Self and the Dramas of History', *Pastoral Psychology*, 9(85): 15–17.

Rogers, C.R. (1959) 'A theory of therapy, personality and interpersonal relationships as developed in the client-centered framework', in S. Koch (ed.), *Psychology: a Study of Science, Vol. III. Formulations of the Person and the Social Context*. New York: McGraw-Hill. pp. 184–256.

Rogers, C.R. (1961) *On Becoming a Person*. Boston: Houghton Mifflin.

Rogers, C.R. (1969) *Freedom to Learn: a View of What Education Might Become*. Columbus, OH: Charles E. Merrill.

Rogers, C.R. (1970) *Carl Rogers on Encounter Groups*. New York: Harper and Row.

Rogers, C.R. (1972) *Becoming Partners: Marriage and its Alternatives*. New York: Delacorte Press.

Rogers, C.R. (1974a) 'In retrospect: forty-six years', *American Psychologist*, 29(2): 115–23.

Rogers, C.R. (1974b) 'Remarks on the future of client-centered therapy', in D. Wexler and L. Rice (eds), *Innovations in Client-Centered Therapy*. New York: John Wiley. pp. 7–13.

Rogers, C.R. (1977) *Carl Rogers on Personal Power*. New York: Delacorte Press.

Rogers, C.R. (1978) 'Do we need *a* reality?', *Dawnpoint*, 1(2): 6–9.

Rogers, C.R. (1980) *A Way of Being.* Boston: Houghton Mifflin.

Rogers, C.R. (1981) 'Some unanswered questions', *Journey,* 1(1): 1, 4.

Rogers, C.R. (1982) 'Reply to Rollo May's letter', *Journal of Humanistic Psychology,* 22(4): 85–9.

Rogers, C.R. (1985) 'Toward a more human science of the person', *Journal of Humanistic Psychology,* 25(4): 7–24.

Rogers, C.R. (1986a) 'Carl Rogers on the development of the person-centered approach', *Person-Centered Review,* 1(3): 257–9.

Rogers, C.R. (1986b) 'A client-centered/person-centered approach to therapy', in I.L. Kutash and A. Wolf (eds), *Psychotherapist's Casebook.* San Francisco: Jossey-Bass. pp. 197–208.

Rogers, C.R. (1986c) 'Rogers, Kohut and Erickson: a personal perspective on some similarities and differences', *Person-Centered Review* 1(2): 125–40.

Rogers, C.R. (1986d) 'Reflection of feelings', *Person-Centered Review,* 1(4): 375–7.

Rogers, C.R. (1987) 'Comment on Shlien's article "A countertheory of transference"', *Person-Centered Review,* 2(2): 182–8.

Rogers, C.R. and Dymond, R.F. (eds) (1954) *Psychotherapy and Personality Change.* Chicago: University of Chicago Press.

Rogers, C.R. and Sanford, R.C. (1989) 'Client-centered psychotherapy' in H.I. Kaplan and B.J. Sadock (eds), *Comprehensive Textbook of Psychiatry,* V. Baltimore: Williams & Wilkins. pp. 1482–501.

Shlien, J.M. (1984) 'A countertheory of transference', in R.F. Levant and J.M. Shlien (eds), *Client-Centered Therapy and the Person-Centered Approach.* New York: Praeger. pp. 153–81.

Shostrom, E. (ed.) (1965) *Three Approaches to Psychotherapy: Client-Centered Therapy.* Film production. Orange, CA: Psychological Films.

Standal, S. (1954) 'The need for positive regard: a contribution to client-centered theory'. Doctoral dissertation, University of Chicago.

Taft, J. (1958) *Otto Rank.* New York: Julian Press.

Tausch, R. (1978) 'Facilitative dimensions in interpersonal relations: verifying the theoretical assumptions of Carl Rogers in school, family education, client-centered therapy and encounter groups', *College Student Journal,* 12: 2–11.

Tausch, R. (1990) 'The supplementation of client-centered communication therapy with other validated therapeutic methods: a client-centered necessity', in G. Lietaer, J. Rombauts and R. Van Balen (eds), *Client-Centered and Experiential Psychotherapy in the Nineties.* Leuven: Leuven University Press. pp. 448–55.

Temaner Brodley, B. (1988) 'Re-examination of client-centered therapy using Rogers' tapes and films'. From panel discussion on client-centered therapy, Symposium at the meeting of the American Psychological Association, Atlanta.

Temaner Brodley, B. (1990) 'Client-centered and experiential: two different therapies', in G. Lietaer, J. Rombauts and R. Van Balen (eds), *Client-Centered and Experiential Psychotherapy in the Nineties.* Leuven: Leuven University Press. pp. 87–107.

Temaner Brodley, B. (1991) 'Some observations of Carl Rogers' verbal behaviour in therapy interviews'. Unpublished presentation at the Second International Conference on Client-Centred and Experiential Psychotherapy, University of Stirling, Scotland.

Thorne, B.J. (1985) *The Quality of Tenderness.* Norwich: Norwich Centre Publications.

Thorne, B.J. (1988) 'The person-centred approach to large groups', in M. Aveline and W. Dryden (eds), *Group Therapy in Britain*. Milton Keynes: Open University Press. pp. 185–207.

Thorne, B.J. (1990) 'Carl Rogers and the doctrine of original sin', *Person-Centered Review*, 5(4): 394–405.

Van Balen, R. (1990) 'The therapeutic relationship according to Carl Rogers: only a climate? A dialogue? Or both?', in G. Lietaer, J. Rombauts and R. Van Balen (eds), *Client-Centered and Experiential Psychotherapy in the Nineties*. Leuven: Leuven University Press. pp. 65–85.

Van Belle, H. (1980) *Basic Intent and Therapeutic Approach of Carl Rogers*. Toronto: Wedge Publishing Foundation.

Vitz, P. (1977) *Psychology as Religion: the Cult of Self-Worship*. Grand Rapids, MI: William B. Eerdmans.

Watson, N. (1984) 'The empirical status of Rogers's hypotheses of the necessary and sufficient conditions for effective psychotherapy', in R.F. Levant and J.M. Shlien (eds), *Client-Centered Therapy and the Person-Centered Approach*. New York: Praeger. pp. 17–40.

Wood, J.K. (1986) 'Roundtable discussion', *Person-Centered Review*, 1(3): 350–1.

Yeoman, L. (1991) 'Calvinism, conversion and the person-centred approach'. Unpublished presentation at the Second International Conference on Client-Centred and Experiential Psychotherapy, University of Stirling, Scotland.

Index